World University Library

The World University Library is an international series
of books, each of which has been specially commissioned.
The authors are leading scientists and scholars from all over
the world who, in an age of increasing specialization, see the
need for a broad, up-to-date presentation of their subject.
The aim is to provide authoritative introductory books for
students which will be of interest also to the general
reader. Publication of the series takes place in Britain,
France, Germany, Holland, Italy, Spain, Sweden and
the United States.

The Inspiration of the poet by Poussin
(about 1630). Musée du Louvre.

Raymond Picard

Two Centuries of French Literature

Translated by John Cairncross

c 1

World University Library

McGraw-Hill Book Company
New York Toronto

Phototypeset by BAS Printers Limited, Wallop, Hampshire, England
Manufactured by LIBREX, Italy.

Contents

Foreword

The reader will hardly expect in two hundred and fifty pages the history of two extraordinarily rich and original centuries of French literature. Nor should he look for a comprehensive survey of that literature. If I were to cover the whole ground adopting a chronological, dialectical or panoramic approach, I would in fact be reducing the work to an empty enumeration and not really be talking about anything at all. For the present venture to be meaningful, I have been repeatedly obliged to make a choice – and an arbitrary one at that. Naturally I could explain each of these choices in detail, but I would not be able fully to justify them. For the very idea of choice cannot be justified, since the reader should really go through, understand and appreciate the whole of French literature. It may therefore be a matter for regret, though not astonishment, if I have dealt with Pascal and La Bruyère but not with Descartes, La Rochefoucauld, Bossuet or Fénelon; with Malherbe and La Fontaine but not with Théophile, Racan, Tristan or Boileau; with Marivaux the novelist but not with Challes, Crébillon, Restif or Sade; and that there are a few words about Voltaire the historian but nothing about Saint Simon.

Even the authors included have been given a dangerously concise treatment. What can be said of Laclos in barely five pages, or of Rousseau in fifteen? I have had to confine myself to the essentials. But what *are* the essentials? It seemed to me that, for the non-specialist reader of today, French literature is basically composed of a number of works, not neatly classified in the pigeonholes of this or that philosophy, but lining the shelves of our libraries – works that have survived and been constantly re-edited because they are still capable of enriching and giving pleasure to the reader. I therefore made little use of literary archaeology and concentrated on that part of French literature of two or three centuries ago which belongs in our civilised twentieth-century heritage, where it is still very much alive. I have thus tried to put myself in the place of the reader coming fresh to the subject, and have had no trouble in recapturing his unspoilt delight and zest.

To help the reader of good will, I have tried to supply the information needed for him to reconnoitre each of the works, to place them in an historical perspective, and above all in a *literary* one, for it is a dangerous illusion to imagine that historical background alone is sufficient for an understanding of literature. I have related the works of the different types of style then current. While drawing on the latest research, I have avoided the biographical or historical anecdote which schematises a work into the fruit of a particular life or epoch. And still more I have rejected the dreary approach which turns the work into a mere illustration of an ideology or into a specimen of the fashionable aesthetic classification – be it classical, baroque, mannerist or anything else. These labels explain nothing, and are more likely to prove misleading.

What I have done is to seek out the literary significance, that is, the relation between the psychology, philosophy and morals inherent in the text, and the feel and colour of the style. Accordingly the texts have been allowed to speak for themselves wherever possible. In this connexion, the conception of a literary genre is of particular importance in French literature. In the seventeenth and eighteenth century, literary creation was not the spontaneous and unmotivated outflow of an author's inspiration. It presupposed the deliberate choice of a certain type of work rathèr than another, and the fashioning of this work called for the application of specific techniques and conventions. The product was designed to satisfy certain expectations on the part of the public. In the great majority of cases, the genre forms a convenient framework of reference for the work which, in a host of way, either realises, illuminates, recasts, eludes or mocks the genre's demands.

The present book, it will be clear, is not, despite its brevity and condensation, a work of popularisation. It is based entirely on first-hand knowledge. But I would like to stress that I have decided against a neutral and undifferentiated treatment of the whole field and have deliberately highlighted certain selected aspects of the subject – which does not imply rejection of the others. Moreover, while seeking to remain strictly objective, I have permitted myself certain personal interpretations and I have taken sides as regards certain methodological problems. The themes developed here may seem well-worn and traditional, or on the contrary paradoxical and provocative. It matters little, for nowadays a commonplace and a paradox are practically indistinguishable. I shall be happy if the guidance supplied in the following pages induces the reader to turn or return to the texts and take sides himself.

The layout of the book is simple. For both centuries, a chapter is devoted to each of the main genres. In that chapter, a swift general exposé is followed by a short study of the outstanding authors or works in the main genres involved. In chapter 7 the literature of the eighteenth-century *philosophes* (the writers of the Enlightenment), which covers a very wide range, is examined in four sub-sections, one to each of the four greatest thinkers.

To assist the reader to follow up the broad indications derived from my book, I have given a brief bibliography[1] of the best editions and most useful studies. The references to this bibliography come first in the notes for each section, chapter, author or work; the place of publication is not shown if it is Paris. I have also included the reference in the case of all quotations. In order not to clutter up the text, these are shown in brackets where possible (Roman figures refer to the book or act, Arabic to the chapter or scene, etc.). The notes run continuously throughout the book.

Part 1

The Seventeenth Century

Louis XIV outside the grotto of Thetis
(now destroyed) in the park at Versailles
(about 1682). Musée de Versailles.

1 Religion, philosophy and psychological analysis

The seventeenth century produced a vast literature on spiritual, philosophical and psychological questions[2]. Religion was a factor in the consideration of every type of action. From Saint François de Sales and his *Introduction à la vie dévote* (1609) to Fénelon and his *Maximes des Saints* (1697), whole libraries were inspired by the spirit of edification and the desire to provide matter for theological reflection and spiritual guidance. Preaching, which was particularly important in the second half of the century, rose to great moral and literary heights with Bossuet's panegyrics, sermons and funeral orations.

However, the Church in France was a house divided. There were rivalries between factions or individuals, and differences of opinion over theology and ethics. One of the most resounding controversies was between the Jesuits and the Jansenists of Port-Royal; another was the battle over quietism. The masterpiece of all the literature produced by these polemics was Pascal's eighteen *Provinciales* (1656–7). Under their veneer of deceptive naïveté, they were uproariously funny and bitingly satirical. They were a prodigious success. Moreover, despite the ostensibly universal authority of the Church, the unbelievers – the so-called *libertins* – were legion. The most ingenious attempt to win them over and bring them back to the fold was also due to Pascal, but it was never completed and all that is left of it is his *Pensées*.

Philosophy achieved a relative degree of freedom from religion and gave rise to an admirably fruitful corpus of thought. In 1637 Descartes, one of the founders of modern philosophy, published his *Discours de la Méthode* (in French), and in 1641 his *Méditations* (in Latin). Malebranche's *Recherche de la Vérité* appeared in 1674–5.

But what appealed to the wider public was a more concrete, less systematic and above all more worldly kind of knowledge. Readers' curiosity about themselves was insatiable. A whole literature on psychology and behaviour set out to define and explain virtues and vices, to describe the different types of conduct and to range over a wide gamut of feelings and passions. Scores of writers transmitted the findings of this survey, in the form of contrasting portraits, subtle analyses or brilliant formulas. The two outstanding collections of observations or portraits are La Rochefoucauld's *Maximes* (1665) and La Bruyère's *Caractères* (1688–94).

Lastly, the resulting knowledge of man was turned to account and verified whenever occasion offered in everyday life – whether in correspondence or in politics or in the form of memoirs. Even when letters became less spontaneous and natural, they formed a

subdivided into a large number of species – the *galant,* playful, amatory, informative or travel-oriented, etc. Guez de Balzac made a great name for himself, in the first half of the century, by his skill in handling the technique of letter-writing; but, in the second half, it was Madame de Sévigné who was, and still is, the most striking instance of a writer whose whole life was given shape and structure day in day out in an unceasing correspondence. The equally numerous memoirs were of course designed to achieve an apologetic rather than an historical end. They are notable in particular because of their art of depicting men and passing judgment on them. The most remarkable success of this type was achieved by the Cardinal de Retz (*circa* 1660–75). His *Memoirs* reveal a remarkably penetrating grasp of psychology, and as often as not a consummate draftsmanship.

Pascal's *Pensées*

The *Pensées* are detached reflections and personal jottings designed to constitute a major work which was never in fact written[3]. Published in 1670, that is, six years after Pascal's death, this compilation is thus more or less raw material for a finished work. In an age when

writers greatly valued order, method and composition, it may appear surprising that the *Pensées* were at once hailed as a landmark. And this judgment has stood the test of time. Posthumous interest in the *Pensées* has never flagged.

But it was at once asked what plan Pascal had in mind for the book, and hence in what order the surviving fragments should be edited. Pascal's brother-in-law, who was responsible for the 1670 (Port-Royal) edition, tells us in his preface that Pascal's writings were found 'all clipped together in various bundles, but without any system or continuity because ... they were only the first draft of

his thoughts which he jotted down on scraps of paper as and when they occurred to him'. However, he continues 'The first thing that was done was to copy them out in the same confused order in which they were found'. The old copy has been preserved, and so we know how the material in the bundles (twenty-seven of them) was arranged. These contained about half of the fragments. The rest of the notes was without any kind of order.

Unfortunately, with all its twists and turns, this plan in twenty-seven parts is extremely obscure. It undoubtedly represents only a stage in the evolution of Pascal's work, and there is hardly any point to an edition which merely reproduces this jigsaw puzzle along with the chaotic sequence of the unclassified fragments. The problem has in fact never been solved. It is still one of France's national pastimes (there have been at least a dozen attempts over the past hundred years) to try to reconstruct the original plan of the work envisaged by Pascal and to group the fragments in accordance with

Left Part of the original manuscript of the *Pensées* showing numbers 237 (*partis*), 210, 221 and 190 of the small Brunschvicg edition. The whole manuscript is equally difficult to decipher. The separate fragments were first strung in bundles (notice the holes) before being finally stuck down on to sheets of paper.

Right The first page of the first edition (1669). The motto on the vignette 'The unfinished words are idle' from the Aeneid (book IV, l. 88) emphasises that the work is incomplete. On the right is shown building materials, on the left, a building in course of construction – as the author left his own work – and in the centre the completed church, symbol of the Apologia that Pascal intended but never achieved.

pendent opera interrupta

PENSÉES
DE
M. PASCAL
SUR LA RELIGION,
ET SUR QUELQUES
AUTRES SUJETS.

I.

Contre l'Indifférence des Athées.

QUE ceux qui combattent la Religion apprennent au moins quelle elle est avant que de la combattre. Si cette Religion se vantoit d'avoir une

A

that plan, or, failing that, in a clear and methodical order. The most reasonable course is probably to be content with a methodical presentation such as the one in the Brunschvicg edition, while taking full account of any suggestions by the latest research. But we should not expect to find a conscious and definitive plan, for the simple reason that a plan of this kind cannot possibly exist in the case of a work that was never finished. Pascal is careful to warn his readers that 'The last thing one hits on in writing a work is what to put at the beginning' (19).

If, judging by the various editions, the order in which the *Pensées* are to be presented is still obscure or arbitrary, at least the intention of the projected work is clear. This is to persuade the different kinds of unbelievers of the truth of Christianity. Hence, the *Pensées* must be interpreted by the criteria of the traditional and clearly-defined genre of the apologia. As it is, this has often been lost sight of, and the result has been a series of strange misreadings. The romantic and feverish figure of Pascal, the sick genius whose cries of anguish were the expression of his metaphysical disquiet, is partly attributable to the false perspective in which his *Pensées* have been viewed. In an age of exhibitionism, of confessions, of intimate journals, people have been misled by the title *Pensées,* imagining that they were noted down whenever they came to mind, which would explain the lack of order. Even Paul Valéry, who had no illusions about the glamour of romantic lyricism, is guilty of this error. He reproaches Pascal with having exclaimed in a famous *Pensée* 'The silence of these eternal spaces terrifies me' (206), and indeed, if Pascal is a believer, why is he so terrified? 'This Christian', Valéry observes, 'does not see his Father in heaven.'[4] But it is not Pascal who is speaking thus: it is the unbeliever, the *libertin,* whom he is using for the purposes of his demonstration and in whose mouth he is entitled to place these anguished words since, for the unbeliever, *Our Father in heaven* does not exist. It is a mistake to imagine, as is still too often the case, that Pascal was daily visited by the vertigo, the terror, the inner wretchedness which he describes. He has given an extraordinarily vivid and convincing picture, in a Christian perspective, of the state of the man who does not believe in God and who is abandoned to his own corrupt nature. But Pascal himself felt that he was redeemed, and his love of God made him shed 'tears of joy'[5]. The despair exuded by the *Pensées* is not Pascal's own despair. If he were overwhelmed by such a feeling, he would not succeed so well in giving such an account of it. For there is a sort of theatrical projection of anguish in the *Pensées*. Valéry saw in Pascal a character out of Shakespeare. 'Custom has made of him', said that writer, 'a kind of French Jansenist Hamlet who weighs his own skull – a great geometrician's skull, and who shudders and dreams dreams on a terrace looking out on the universe. He is swept by the biting wind of the infinite; and he talks to himself on the margin of the void where he makes his appearance exactly as if he were in the front of a stage; he reasons in the presence of all and sundry with his own spectre.' But, in this drama, Pascal is not one of the cast. He is the producer.

What he sets out to do is to make the unbelievers feel that their situation is untenable. In most cases, they do not realise it, for they slumber in a tranquil indifference to their salvation. 'This peace of mind in this state of ignorance is something monstrous, the absurdity and stupidity of which must be brought home to those who spend their life in it by demonstrating its existence to them in order to confound them by the spectacle of their folly.' (195). It is essential to awaken them as quickly as possible, to make them aware of their wretchedness of which they have not the slightest idea, to upset and terrify them, and to cast them into a despair from which faith alone, or the expectation of faith, can retrieve them. Accordingly Pascal, the fisherman of souls, uses psychological, literary and poetical devices to construct a despair which is a kind of trap to catch the unbelievers. He cuts the ground from under their feet, plunges them into an unstable and shifting world, and finally launches them into the dizzying realm of the infinite. 'We sail along in the vast middle reaches – always wavering and drifting, buffeted from one extreme to the other, with no fixed point. At whatever destination we may plan to moor or ensconce ourselves, it gives way and abandons us, and, if we go after it, it evades our grasp, slips away from us and flees with an eternal flight.' (72).

The literary artifice in the rhythm and in the final cadence is evident as soon as we stand back and take a look at this admirable passage in perspective. The *Pensées* on style, eloquence and the art of persuasion (i.e. rhetoric) show clearly how deeply Pascal had reflected on the potential contribution of literature and psychology in the genre of the apologia. And, well aware as he was of the diversity of minds, vocations and attitudes, he orchestrated a whole range of dramatic demonstrations, suiting their weight and argument to the type of a believer whom he had in mind. Obviously, one and the same approach will not reduce to despair both a scholar and a man of the world. The former must be persuaded that knowledge is unattainable and the latter must be shown the hollowness and absurdity of his life.

The *Pensées,* then, offer a many-sided and gripping picture of the state of man abandoned to his own devices and to his natural impotence, of the creature cut off from the Creator, in short, plunged in what Pascal calls 'the wretchedness of man without God'. Even man's physical situation in the universe is intolerable. He walks a dizzy tightrope between the vast infinity of astronomy revealed by the telescope, and the tiny infinity in the world of biology disclosed by the microscope, that is, 'between these two abysses of infinity and nothingness'. And, in the order of intelligible things, 'his intelligence has the same rank as [his] body in the extension of nature'. He is therefore, 'equally incapable of seeing the void from which he has emerged and the infinite in which he is engulfed'. He must be content with 'perceiving [some] appearance of the middle range of things, in an eternal despair at knowing neither the principle underlying them nor their end'(72). Man is incapable of knowledge. Besides, our senses deceive us. We are governed by imagination, 'mistress of error and falsehood' (82). Custom, which is nothing else than the perpetuation of error, imposes its prejudices on us. And, since it is not possible to attain truth, opinions are contradictory. 'Truth this side of the Pyrenees; error on the other'. (294). Men of the world, who are left indifferent by the bankruptcy of science and philosophy, are no better off, for they are a prey to boredom. 'Man finds nothing so unbearable as to be completely at rest, without passions, without occupations, without recreation, without an aim. It is then that he feels his nothingness, his state of abandonment, his inadequacy, his emptiness. Straightway there will rise within his soul tedium, melancholy, sadness, grief, spite, despair.' (131). It is the need to escape from tedium, even by the most stupid activities, which largely explains society and social life. Man cannot 'stay quiet in a room', for there he would be face to face with himself and he would become aware of his 'feeble and mortal state which is so wretched that nothing can console us when we consider it closely' (139). He therefore seeks by every possible means to turn aside from this thought and to hurl himself into a round of diversions. 'As men have not found the remedy for death, wretchedness and ignorance, they have hit on the idea of not thinking of them at all, in order to keep themselves happy.' This is the real origin of gambling, hunting and also of war, dancing and conversation, the different occupations and even the organisation of society. For the great advantage of being a secretary of state, a chancellor or the king consists in not having an instant to think of oneself. In gambling, the real aim is not the winnings, nor the quarry in hunting, nor victory in war. What people want is to escape from themselves. Men spend 'the whole day in the pursuit of a hare which they would not dream of buying' (139) or in driving a ball across a billiard table. But these occupations are not only of a distressing futility. This derisory effort of men to escape from the realisation of their wretchedness is the very proof of that wretchedness. 'How hollow is the heart of man and how full of filth.' (143).

Social and political life offers a spectacle which confirms this despairing judgment. As man is incapable of distinguishing between truth and falsehood, he cannot decide what is right and fair. In any case, it is might that reigns in this world, and justice cannot make its voice heard, for 'might has contradicted justice and has announced that might is right; and so, not having been able to make what is right strong, we have made what is strong right' (298). Laws and régimes are therefore what might has made them, and custom preserves them until might calls them in question again. But it matters little, for human society is 'like a lunatic asylum' (331), and there is nothing to choose between governments since none of them is worth a jot. Given that absurdity is universal, we must bear with the existing régime rather than have recourse to might which, after considerable bloodshed, would in the end set up a régime no whit better. The monarchical system governing succession to the throne is admittedly absurd. 'What could be less reasonable than to choose the son of a queen to govern a state? To steer a ship we do not choose the passenger who is of the best family.' (320). But whom is one to choose? The most virtuous and the most skilful? 'At once we come to blows, for everyone claims to be the most virtuous and skilful. Let us therefore attach this quality to something that cannot give rise to dispute. It is the King's eldest son. This is clear; there is no dispute. Reason cannot do better, for civil war is the greatest evil' (320). The laws must therefore be obeyed, not because they are just, 'but because they are the laws' (325), and the government, not because it is good but because it is in power. In an age of monarchy by divine right, Pascal explains the personal prestige of kings by a kind of conditioned reflex of the people, accustomed as it is to see kings 'accompanied by guards, drums, officers and all the things which force the human frame to bow to respect and terror' (308). He firmly repudiates religious explanations, excludes communities (e.g. nations) as such from redemption and constructs a positivist, realistic and cynical system in the line of Machiavelli and Hobbes.

In Pascal's *Apologie de la religion chrétienne* it is the individual and social situation of unredeemed man which continues to obsess readers today. The famous picture is unforgettable: 'Let us imagine a number of men in chains, all of them condemned to death, some of whom are slaughtered every day before the others' eyes. Those left alive see their own fate in that of their fellow prisoners, and, looking at each other sorrowfully and hopelessly, they wait their turn. This is the image of the state of man' (199). It is certainly the 'sublime misanthrope'[6], as Voltaire, in an intentional misrepresentation, put it, the lucid and cruel observer whose presence is still most acutely felt today. The logician too, for, with his inversion of the pro to the contra, he gives an admirable example of the dialectical method: 'The two opposing reasons', he writes. 'We must begin with that. Without that we cannot understand anything and everything is heretical. And indeed, at the end of each proposition, we must add that we are mindful of the opposite proposition.' (567). Whether as a dialectician or as a painter, Pascal makes us feel, with almost unbearable intensity, what it is to be abandoned. It is clear that Antoine Roquentin, Sartre's hero in *La Nausée*, moves in a Pascalian universe. Men, he explains, take refuge in diversion in order to escape from their horror of existing. 'They all have their pet little complaint which prevents them from realising that they exist . . . [But I] have no worries, I have money, like a rentier, no boss, no wife or children; I exist, that's all . . . Now when I say *I*, it has a hollow ring . . . And who is this Antoine Roquentin? It's abstract stuff.' It is precisely in the *Pensées* that we find this same modern awareness of the unsubstantiality of the ego and the anguish on which existential experience is based.

However, as we have seen, the portrayal of man's wretchedness was for Pascal only a stage in his apologetics, and indeed he felt that it was unwise to dwell too long on it. 'It is dangerous to show man too clearly how like the animals he is without showing him his greatness as well.' (418). Now man, in his very wretchedness, is great because he is aware of it. 'It is to be great to know that one is wretched . . . A tree does not know that it is wretched.' (397). Man has this sad but stimulating privilege, and 'all man's dignity consists of thought' (365). Admittedly thought remains ineffective, for its functioning is hampered by deceptive powers. Besides, 'man is not guided by reason, which is his essential attribute' (491). But,

La Bruyère, Ménalque, *Caractères* XI, 7. The absent-minded man 'holds a box of dice in one hand and a glass in the other and as he is very thirsty he swallows the dice and nearly the box as well, throws the glass of water on the backgammon board and drenches the person he is playing with'.
(Engraving by Gravelot for the 1765 edition.)

even within the limits of his fallen nature, he retains a sort of infallible instinct which reveals God to him, as well as the elementary principles of geometry. This is knowledge through what Pascal calls the *heart*. In fact, 'what nature is in animals we call wretchedness in man [who thus feels that he has] fallen off from a better nature which was once a part of him' (409). The feeling of wretchedness is the proof of the Fall and of the need for redemption. The unbeliever is induced to seek to believe, and Pascal then provides him with all the arguments capable of convincing him. The Apology achieves its aim, which was the conversion of the freethinker. But many readers part company with Pascal before he comes to the end of his journey. They will accept only his pitiless analysis of the state of man. The influence of the *Pensées* on western civilisation is not so much apologetic as philosophical.

La Bruyère's *Caractères*

La Bruyère is a one-book man. He is always identified with *Les Caractères ou les Moeurs de ce Siècle*[7]. What is more, at first sight this book is not even by him at all. Right from its appearance in 1688, it purported to be merely a translation and continuation of the *Characters* by Theophrastes. But, as one edition followed another, and La Bruyère added to his own text, the translation of the Greek philosopher rapidly came to form only a small part of the volume. For example, in the seventh edition (1692) Theophrastes is given fifty-four pages of small print as against six hundred and twenty-five, set in the main type-size, for La Bruyère himself. Thus, despite the modesty of the author, who makes a point of hiding behind the classical writer (a frequent seventeenth-century device), this is an original work on the behaviour, attitudes, vices, failings and prejudices of the time, and La Bruyère, with every year that passed, expanded his hoard of observations, remarks, judgments and

LES
CARACTERES
DE
LA BRUYERE.

E rends au public ce qu'il m'a prêté : j'ai emprunté de lui la matiere de cet ouvrage, il eſt juſte que l'ayant achevé avec toute l'attention pour la vérité dont je ſuis capable, & qu'il mérite de moi, je lui en faſſe la reſtitution. Il peut regarder avec loiſir ce portrait que j'ai fait de lui d'après nature ; & s'il ſe connoît quelques-uns des défauts que je touche, s'en corriger. C'eſt l'unique fin que l'on doit ſe propoſer en écrivant, & le ſuccès auſſi que l'on doit moins ſe promettre. Mais comme les hommes ne ſe dégoutent point du vice, il ne faut pas auſſi ſe laſſer de le leur reprocher : ils ſeroient peut-être pires, s'ils venoient à manquer de cenſeurs ou de critiques ; c'eſt ce qui fait que l'on prêche, & que

K

portraits. In 1688 there were four hundred and twenty. In 1694 (his last edition) they numbered 1,120. In any case, as was pointed out by perceptive readers, 'the subject matter is ... inexhaustible [... and] not a year goes by without the follies of men furnishing you with a volume'[8].

The huge success of such a work, despite its ill-defined scope and at times rather rambling pace, is due not only to the scandal arising from certain identifications but also and above all to the intense interest (going back half a century) of a whole section of the public in the study of psychology and conduct. The men of the age were convinced that behaviour was fundamentally intelligible. Despite its variety, its complexity and its contradictions, it constituted a stable and homogeneous field of study. It could be described; its manifestations could be classified, perhaps even form the basis for deduction[9]. There were universal judgments, rules which were applicable to every possible case. The diversity of minds, feelings

La Carte du Tendre, engraved by Chauveau in 1654
for the first volume of Mlle de Scudéry's novel
Clélie. In a spirit which contemporaries found
witty, it charts the various attitudes and feelings
the characters in the novel pass through
in the course of their amorous quest.

and attitudes could be reduced to general and constant patterns which it was possible to determine and in terms of which, with an adequate dose of subtlety, individual anomalies could be satisfactorily defined. In short, they practised what we would today call an *essentialist* psychology, and they disserted on friendship or vanity as if they were moral substances possessing specific properties. When publishing a collection of verse by different hands in 1665, a friend of Madame de Sévigné's felt that the most convenient way of listing the different forms of love was to put them in alphabetical order with a view, as he explained, 'to bringing some tidiness into such diversity'[10]. The passages thus quoted were classified under clearly defined rubrics, and the reader moved from *Despite* to *Desire,* and then from *Disorder of the Heart* to *Discordance.* In a word, there was a sort of transcription of the moral world into spatial terms. The *Carte du Tendre* had already given a geographical contour to the inevitable stages of one form of love[11]. In the same way La Bruyère takes his reader through the maze of a psychological garden, describing and assessing the various clumps of shrubs and the innumerable species, passing from the gentleman *(honnête homme)* to the well-bred man (*l'homme de bien*), from the man of good sense to the man of good taste, and from the fool to the conceited fop.

But a careful distinction must be made between them. For it is important to identify those species which are so closely related as to be mistaken for each other, to separate what seems to belong together, and lastly to pinpoint differences which had only been vaguely noted. There is in La Bruyère a sort of naturalist who catalogues and observes the peculiarities of psychological life. And it is no accident that he has put himself under the patronage of Theophrastes. A disciple of Aristotle, the Greek philosopher was the author of treatises on botany, meteorology, physics and zoology, and in his treatise on *Characters* he applies the same method of classification and observation to the study of manners. The character is the distinctive mark which enables us to recognise a particular nature, which in effect characterises it. But at this point science becomes something of a sport. The identification of the decisive sign presupposed an effort to make distinctions which become more and more subtle as each analyst sought to outbid the other. For the tendency was to discover increasingly imperceptible variations and delicate shades. A survey of this kind naturally gave rise to a drawing-room diversion in which everyone was able to show off his ingenuity. The *portrait* which, by constant retouching, built up to a specific individuality and the *maxim* which brought out an illuminating and previously unsuspected connection between different concepts of conduct were genres which flourished in the salons and from there soon invaded the whole field of literature.

However, instead of degenerating into mechanical and conventional exercises, these analyses made possible, within clearly determined limits, a veritable campaign of psychological exploration. The inherent brevity of the maxim encouraged research into modes of expression. The selectiveness and the precision demanded by the portrait stimulated not only observation but a sort of algebra of concepts of behaviour. Strangely enough, it fell to La Bruyère in the quiet of his study to devote his efforts to these diversions which had so long been the preserve of society circles, to impart to them a high degree of variety, explaining the subjects to be studied by, in turn as he puts it 'a definition, a maxim, an argument, a parallel, a straight-forward comparison, a trait, a description or a painting'[12] and to present his discoveries to the public under the title of *The Characters or The Manners of the Present Century*.

Can the work be regarded as a coherent whole with a logical structure? It certainly cannot. La Bruyère admits that he has studied man 'haphazardly, unmethodically, as and when the subject came up – by age, sex and station, and by the vices, foibles and ridiculousness attaching to each of them'[13]. The order of the reflections is not often very enlightening and sometimes frankly capricious and arbitrary. Between one edition and the next, dozens of new pieces were inserted, while others were sometimes switched from one chapter to another. But, if there is little hope of ever deciphering a hidden or mysterious sequence which might explain the position of each of the 1,120 remarks, the fact remains that the ingredients of this carefully put together work are very far from random. La Bruyère, the least negligent of men, was at pains to achieve the desired effects of contrast and echo. It is obvious, to take only one example, that the opening remark in the first chapter *Des ouvrages de l'esprit*, 'Everything has been said, and we come too late', corresponds to the last one (69): 'Horace or Boileau said so before you. Yes, I take your word for it, but I have said it in my own special way'.

The first ten chapters study life, customs, institutions – the *Ouvrages de l'esprit* first of all, since the contemporaries' interest in these was unbounded and since the writer was induced to reflect on his own undertaking in the process. Then follows *Du mérite personnel,* of value only if it is based on the genuine qualities of mind and heart, though in real life this is never the case. Next there are two chapters on the fair sex and on the feelings which they inspire – one of the ruling powers in polite society, *Des femmes* and *Du coeur.* Chapter v – *De la société et de la conversation* – is devoted to society life. Lastly, five chapters review the five social categories whose role at that time was decisive and the principles underlying each of them – the world of money with its maniacs and its victims (*Des biens de fortune*); *De la Ville,* that is, Paris society; *De la Cour*; aristocracy and birth (*Des Grands*); and the monarch (*Du souverain ou de la république*). This social gradation culminates in the King, to whom La Bruyère erects a statue at the end of Chapter x. His survey then becomes less closely linked with the structure of the society of the age, less involved in history. It turns off sharply to concentrate on the study of man, as is fairly clear from the titles of the chapters – *De l'homme* (XI); *Des jugements* (XII); *De la mode* (XIII); *De quelques usages* (XIV). By a natural transition, it ends on religion as it is preached *(De la chaire)* and as it is lived *(Des esprits forts)*. The first fifteen chapters have shown the ridiculousness, the void and the absurdity of man. They prepared the way for the sixteenth and last chapter in which man turns to God.

This progression, consciously slanted but extremely subtle, is admirably suited to a student of human behaviour who detests the systematic approach. Despite his preference for universals, La Bruyère is not a philosopher in the modern meaning of the word with a comprehensive and integrated interpretation of man, or of his powers and his position in the world. Nor, despite his naturalist's attitude, is he a scholar concerned with complete enumerations *à la Descartes*. Certain general ideas emerge from his book – of the vanity (i.e. the unsubstantiality, the emptiness) of man, the predominance of personal interest, egoism and self-love, and hypocrisy. But the ideas are not original, since they immediately remind one (and indeed reminded the author himself) of Pascal's *Pensées*, La Rochefoucauld's *Maximes* and Molière's comedies. Above all, he is content to prove their existence by reference to real life, without attempting to make a more thorough analysis or founding a real science of man on it. He is bitter and disillusioned, but his lucid, detached pessimism prompts him to make ill-tempered sallies and not to preach a philosophy of despair.

'A man who is Christian and French by birth', he noted, 'has his hands tied when it comes to satire. He is forbidden to deal with the major topics.' (I, 65). A student of human nature is bound to feel the same embarrassment (and for the same reasons) as a satirist. Devout Christian as he was, La Bruyère did not suffer too much from the restrictions that a state religion imposed on freedom of expression where religion was concerned. His social and political criticism, on the contrary, was undoubtedly influenced by the fact that, as a Frenchman, he lived under the Absolute Monarchy. His daring was great, but it was always slightly muted. He did not go to the bitter end. If he was hard on the grandees and poked fun at the courtiers, it was simply the better to sing the king's praises – or at least to extol the royal dignity. He has forceful pages on the absurdity of war. 'If you were told that all the cats in a great country assembled on a plain', he writes, 'and that, after having mewed to their hearts' content, they fell at each other furiously, and wielded both tooth and claw, that this encounter cost both sides nine or ten thousand cats dead on the field, who infected the air ten leagues round about with the stench . . . [and if these cats] told you that they loved glory, would you conclude that they sought it by assembling at this fine tryst, by destroying each other in this way and wiping out their own species?' (XII, 119). But in another passage he criticises the generals for dining too lavishly during their campaigns – as if there were anything in common between this fairly minor abuse and the catastrophic institution of war. The fact is that La Bruyère, in his inventory of habits and customs, makes no attempt to see the objects he is examining in perspective or to assign these their respective importance in the universe which they combine to form. He is content to let his eye dwell on them for a time. Then he passes by, and we pass by with him.

If he has not sought to carve out and construct an organised world, that does not make him a mere chronicler of day-to-day events, or a purveyor of anecdotes. On the contrary, he is always anxious to rise above the particular, to extract the typical, significant aspects from the individual person or case. True, his taste for the concrete seems to become more marked; from one edition to the next, the number of portraits increases considerably. It rises from a dozen in 1688 to about a hundred and forty in 1694. But, even when he has a living model, what he sees in that model is above all the psychological, moral or social species to which it belongs, and his painting is equally valid for other members of the same species. It is easy to understand why his contemporaries suggested so many *keys* for the portraits in which everybody could recognise himself. *Menippus* is perhaps the Marshal de Villeroy, but he is also the vain and insignificant man of the world. At Versailles such men were legion, and each of them could imagine – unless his friends imagined it for him – that La Bruyère had him in mind. People recognised *Hermippus* as the Count de Villayer, but in reality the type of behaviour in question is to be met with in every century. He is the type who loves to potter about and to have his comforts. In any case, the writer often proceeds by juxtaposing characteristics drawn from a number of individuals, and out of these he composes a sort of generic image. For example, in the case of *Menalcus,* the typically absent-minded man, details are piled on so thick that the portrait becomes completely unconvincing. 'This', he was to note, 'is less a particular character than a collection of facts about absent-mindedness.' The truth is that the reader is almost always confronted not with real portraits, but with what artists today call composite works. La Bruyère, then, is as far (or almost as far) removed from the immediate data of life as from philosophical thought. He moves in the world of conduct which is in between, but is closer to the anarchy of the world than to a transparent and orderly cosmos. His unflagging curiosity for people, for their relationships, for the life they lead is precisely what for two centuries (i.e. up to the *Physiologies* of 1840–2, up to Balzac) gave rise in France to a whole literature of psychological analysis in which we find the same sense of observation, occasionally the same humour, the same concern for precise detail, the same predilection for classifications, the absence, too, of great ideas and of systems, the same rejection of synthesis – a literature which rises above the day-to-day recording of facts, but does not soar into the thoroughly suspect empyrean of doctrine.

In any case, La Bruyère realises that he is not a profound or original thinker. But, since 'everything has been said', the writer can at least strive to put in a striking formula what has already been said. In a slightly modified form, Valéry's dictum 'doubt leads to form'[14] is applicable in this context. Since he will not or cannot be a philosopher, the author of the *Caractères* becomes a stylist. He chooses his terms, polishes his sentences, constructs his paragraphs with meticulous care, makes his effects converge on the objective. This kind of studied effort must occasionally leave traces of stiffness or constraint. The analyst is also a man of letters, and it is no coincidence that his first chapter is devoted to the *Ouvrages de l'esprit*. This feeling of definitive form which he often gives readers is due as much to the perfection of his style as to the accuracy of his aim, and it is hard to say whether the felicity of his touch belongs to the domain of language or to that of psychology. A concerted and many-faceted work, the *Caractères* are both a collection of documents and a repertory of literary exercises. It is the society of Louis XIV seen through the eyes of a man of letters, but in the perspective of eternal man and of eternal literature.

2 Poetry in
the seventeenth century

The concept of poetry in the seventeenth century[15] merged so completely in that of literary creation that it included even works in prose. A contemporary called Honoré d'Urfé's famous novel the poem of *Astrée*[16]. But of course literary achievement *par excellence* was in verse. Here again, however, the term 'poem' was used to designate works which, as is sometimes forgotten nowadays, were above all poetic. A tragedy was usually referred to as a dramatic poem, and it should be remembered that anyone who was then called a poet was just as likely to be a dramatist as a writer of odes and sonnets. Verse was highly esteemed and was cultivated throughout the whole century. There was therefore a vast output of poetry. The works of over two hundred poets have come down to us, and we may rest assured that a large number of compositions which were never published have been lost.

The poetic riches which have survived (some of them still practically unknown) are not, in their almost infinite diversity, the confused outcome of an anarchistic burst of creation. They bear the stamp of certain types of inspiration, and of genres and poetic forms which are in each case defined by conventions, laws and rules. Religious poetry has not the same mood, the same music or the same tone as poems for official occasions or light verse. The epic has its own laws which are not the same as those for the ode or the elegy. The sonnet, the rondeau and the madrigal each follow the rules which define the form of the poem, and these specific factors – tone, genre and form – are superimposed on each other and are combined in, say, a religious sonnet, an official ode or a playful rondeau. Thus, the poets do not abandon themselves unreservedly to their feelings or to the caprice of their poetic verve – the *caprice* itself is a poetic genre. They operate within a definite framework and are governed by the discipline of a particular diction. All these constraints may reduce poetry to the level of an uninventive handicraft or even to petty intellectual diversions – riddles or *bouts-rimés* – which were all the rage in the salons; they may on the other hand, thanks to the effort needed to submit to them and as a result of the difficulties to be overcome, give the poem unusual power, depths and richness.

Critics have tried to account for the many contrasting aspects of the poetry of this age by organising it according to concepts which are accepted or rejected according to which way the wind of fashion is blowing. Thus, poets have been defined as classic, pre-classic, grotesque, out of date, non-conformist, burlesque, independent, precious, baroque, mannerist and so on, and each critic groups the whole output of the century under two or three of these headings. The only one of these categories known to the period is the burlesque, the meaning of which is precisely defined within very narrow limits. The term of precious itself was hardly ever applied to poetry at the time. In fact all these vague, over-simplified labels are dangerous. The expressions mannerist and baroque, borrowed from the graphic or plastic arts and from architecture, have the additional disadvantage that they imply a highly questionable transposition of the arts to literature. The twisted column is a feature of baroque, but what is the poetic form which corresponds to it? There has never been a serious study of the poetic texts. If a determined, unprejudiced analysis were carried out, with no attempt to justify an *a priori* classification, it would be possible to work out a more precise concept of this poetry – a very different one from the prevailing notion – and of the literary conventions which were widely adopted throughout the century. We would then be in a better position to assess the fundamental originality of each of the poets in question, many of whom are indistinguishable at first sight – in much the same way as all Chinese look alike to the ignorant European.

Of the main genres, religious poetry was cultivated by scores of writers – from Malherbe, with his three paraphrases of the Psalms (between 1600 and 1627) to Racine's four *Cantiques Spirituels* (1694) via Corneille's translation in verse of the *Imitation of Christ* (1652–6) and Brébeuf's fine *Entretiens Solitaires* (1660). In a spirit of humility, they have sought to achieve a faithful rendering of the thought, and indeed in many cases of the letter as well, of the religious writings which inspire them. For them, poetry has really become a spiritual exercise. Their abnegation has yielded a rich harvest of admirable verse, and they fulfil all the conditions for the creation of a kind of *poésie pure*.

The composition of a French epic is a dream that goes back for centuries. It was more than ever to the fore from 1653 to 1657. These five years saw the publication of over fifty thousand lines of epic verse. At times dramatic, at times allegorical, these large, somewhat lumbering constructions occasionally burst into flame. Official lyricism, too, in praise of kings and grandees, was cultivated on a lavish scale throughout the century. It brought poets both social prestige and pensions. Malherbe had shown that it could rise to sublime heights. The restoration of order at the beginning of Louis xiv's rule (1659–61) had given it new life and wide scope.

Galant poetry, as light society verse was called, also played a prominent role in literary life. It provided one of the main diversions of the age. Every man of the world regarded it as his duty to be in love (or at least to pay court to a lady), and every lover was a poet (or at least wrote verse). This meant that large numbers of society poems were turned out which brought to light scores of wits and even a few poets.

Lastly, there was serious poetry with epistles and satires of which Boileau was a great exponent, and also fables. Pastoral poetry, too, had its adepts, with his idylls and eclogues, as had elegiac poetry.

A choice among poets so numerous is bound to be arbitrary. If, in entirely different ways, Malherbe and La Fontaine tower above the rest, there is still no good reason for citing Malherbe's two disciples, Maynard and Racan, rather than Théophile de Viau, or Saint-Amant rather than Tristan, Sarasin or Godeau. The lover of

Drawing of Malherbe by Du Monstier. That Malherbe should have sat to Du Monstier, a famous draughtsman of the time, indicates the important position of the official poet at the court of Henri IV. Musée de Chantilly.

poetry must not be content with the anthologies. He should go to the sources themselves where he will find a rich and rewarding variety of little-known poets.

Malherbe

For the last hundred and fifty years or so, poetry in France has been regarded as above all the expression of the poet's inner need. Whether we have in mind the personal lyricism in the manner of the nineteenth-century Romantics or the metaphysical soundings of our contemporaries, the function of poetry now seems to be to render an intimate experience through words or in spite of them.

This concept is far removed from that of Malherbe[17]. What we must look for in his poems is not a cry from the depth of his soul or a more or less ingenuous confession. Nor does he offer us a philosophical revelation, frenzies or even ideas. He was never tempted to abandon himself to facile melodiousness or sentimental effusions. Further, he did not seek to find his true essence or to stammer out his feeling of oneness with the Ultimate. In his eyes, sincerity, profundity and genuineness are not literary values. For him, poetry speaks (or sings) rather than *signifies*; it is first and foremost a matter of diction. The poem is a complex structure of words and sounds, and the poet is its daring architect.

The corpus of precepts and critical remarks which has come down to us under the name of *Malherbian Reformation* deals almost exclusively with versification, grammar and diction. For Boileau, half a century later, the glory of Malherbe consisted in having purified the language, and, 'the first in France'[18], insisted on the observance of certain rules governing the manufacture of verse. In fact Malherbe was very much concerned with euphony. He called for full rhymes. He rigorously banned padding, pleonasms, loose metaphors – all the liberties which the poet takes with traditional meanings and usage. Poetic creation thus became a sort of prodigiously complicated game of patience in which every success presupposed a veritable *tour de force*. In one particular poem, composed of stanzas of ten lines each, and in which each stanza had to be self-contained as regards meaning, the pattern is as follows: first of all a quatrain with alternate feminine and masculine rhymes and ending with a full stop or a semi-colon. Then comes a couplet with feminine rhymes, linked by the meaning to a second quatrain with the first and last lines and the two middle ones rhyming (a/b/b/a). One's head swims when it is remembered that these lines are short (they have only eight syllables), that the caesura is usually after the third foot and that on no account must it be after the fourth foot. In addition, there are the innumerable problems which have to be solved at the same time affecting the choice of words, the harmony and lastly the meaning, which must be as clear and as precise as in prose. The whole structure brings home the futility and ridiculousness of what was thought to be one of the noblest vocations of man. It appears to be extraordinarily difficult to construct a sailing ship in a bottle, but a work of that kind has never been regarded as the supreme achievement of the human mind.

Malherbe himself seems to delight in spreading this kind of disillusionment among students of his works. He pretends to see in poetry nothing more than a gratuitous exercise in virtuosity. He is alleged to have declared 'A good poet [is] no more useful to the State than a good skittles player'. And, in an even more significant utterance, he is supposed to have said to his disciple Racan: 'If our verse lives on after us, all the glory that we may expect is that it may be said of us that we were both outstanding at arranging syllables and that we must have had a great power over words to arrange them so successfully in their right place, and that both of us were quite mad to spend the best years of our life on an exercise that was so little use to the public and to ourselves, instead of employing it on having a good time or on thinking of advancing our fortune'[19].

Of course too much importance must not be attached to these sallies. But at least they show that Malherbe was sometimes able to stand back from the occupation to which he devoted his life, and above all that he had no illusions as to the real interest and the intrinsic value of the difficulties which he had to overcome in order to accomplish his task of 'arranging syllables'. What fascinated him was not this game of manufacturing a mosaic of words. It was the effort, the attention to detail and the rigorous self-control which were necessary if he was to indulge in it. It was also the exquisite and powerful verse which rewarded the unremitting exercise of this discipline. Malherbe praised the literary virtues of constraint. He treated the raw material of language in much the same way as the sculptor uses his marble or the painter his palette. He succeeded in effecting a vigorous fusion of work with art. Poetry so conceived demands an intellectual tension and a lucid painstaking craftsmanship. It is a type of work calling for will-power and reason. His writings, to a much greater degree than those of Molière or Racine, and *a fortiori* those of La Fontaine, provide the basis for a real classicism – an expression which incidentally is unknown to the seventeenth century, and which the nineteenth-century critics so grievously misused. Every one of Malherbe's poems is the miraculous triumph of an ascetic determination which seems almost superhuman. As it is, this demanding poet wrote very little. He is reported to have said that, after a hundred lines, 'one should take ten years off'[20]. There is no doubt but that the never-ending toil which for him was inseparable from poetic creation cost him a great deal of effort and that he only took on the burden out of a sense of duty.

But, if his work is not voluminous, it constitutes an achievement which has rarely been equalled. The midnight oil burned over the composition of the poems has left no trace in his published work. On the contrary, the reader has the impression of complete and effortless smoothness. The public is not called upon to peep into the workshop where the complex process of the manufacture of poetry is carried out. Malherbe himself is reported to have maintained 'that he did not prepare dishes for cooks'[21]. The lover of poetry therefore is confronted with admirable verse which is all the more mysterious for possessing the trite and unaffected clarity of everyday language.

> Beaux et grands bâtiments d'éternelle structure,
> Superbes de matière, et d'ouvrages divers . . .
> Beau parc et beaux jardins, qui dans votre clôture
> Avez toujours des fleurs et des ombrages verts . . .[22]

> (Fair stately pile, eternally renowned,
> Of splendid stone, with various arts arrayed,
> Fair park and gardens fair wherein abound,
> Always bright flowers and always verdant shade) . . .

It is not possible to celebrate more simply and less pompously the palace of Fontainebleau and its gardens. And yet these lines have the same grandeur and the same solidity as the castle which they glorify. The poet has patiently and persistently eliminated one after the other all useless terms – everything unsuitable, out of date or inexact – which he might have been tempted to use. The work is stripped to its essentials. The feeling of something clearcut, firm and definitive that one has in reading Malherbe is the fruit of this resolute refusal to tolerate vagueness or approximation. At the same time he eliminated jarring sounds and associations, a danger which always attends spontaneous writing. He rejected everything that prevented the language from singing. What is left is a full-throated harmony which, paradoxically, seems to emanate from the meaning. One can well imagine that, as Baudelaire puts it, 'a line of Malherbe, symmetrical and foursquare in its melody [can throw one] into prolonged ecstasies'[23]. It seems almost as if language is restored in this poet to its pristine splendour and to its original vocation as a vehicle for music and meaning. It is really the language of the gods – a language of pure quintessences which has yet managed to stay concrete and succulent. The privilege of the poet is to retrieve it, like a gift of nature, from beneath the impurities and the slack, from beneath the corruption with which the common herd has soiled it.

Does this mean that all inspiration is excluded from this arduous labour? Certainly not. But everyone thinks himself a poet, and inspiration is what is lacking least. It is not because one feels the urge to sing, because one is deeply stirred, that one becomes a good poet. Everyone dabbles in verse, and the god of poetry is always easily accessible,

> Apollon, à portes ouvertes,
> Laisse indifféremment cueillir
> Les belles feuilles toujours vertes . . .[24]

> (Apollo opening wide his doors
> Lets each indifferently pluck
> The leaves of splendid evergreen . . .)

from the tree of poetry. 'Indifferently', that is, to all and sundry, without discrimination. But the great poet is one who shows himself capable of constructing a work out of the 'splendid leaves' which inspiration makes available to everyone,

> Mais l'art d'en faire les couronnes
> N'est pas su de toutes personnes.
>
> (But the art of making crowns of them
> Is not possessed by everyone.)

His superiority lies in the science of versifying, in his technique, in a word in the quality of his workmanship. Inspiration is the factor common to all poetry. It is craftsmanship that makes good verse, or, as a contemporary puts it, 'meditation and art'[25].

If poetry is an exercise then, it is not just a gratuitous one. It is always buoyed up by inspiration, and its lyricism has a very elevated function. True, this lyricism is not, as we have seen, devoted to personal revelations. But neither does it consist solely in the tone, in the flowing numbers, in a certain musicality which makes the poem, ode or stanzas, suitable for singing, as it was for the Ancients on the lyre. It also presupposes an outpouring of feeling in which the group and the individual commune. Valéry rightly saw in the religious poetry of the seventeenth century a 'remarkable alliance of collective sentiments, lyrically expressed, with those which proceed from the inner core of the [poet's] personality and faith'[26]. The remark is valid for all forms of lyricism of the age. Malherbe composed only three paraphrases of the Psalms, a genre then in great honour. They are extremely beautiful, and the poet has often caught the plenitude, the power, and the simplicity of biblical lyricism.

La gloire des méchants est pareille à cette herbe
Qui, sans porter jamais ni javelle ni gerbe,
Croît sur le toit pourri d'une vieille maison;
On la voit séche et morte aussitôt qu'elle est née
     Et vivre une journée
Est réputé pour elle une longue saison.[27]

(The wicked's glory is like that of grass
Which, never bearing either swathe or sheaf,
Grows on an ancient mansion's mouldering roof;
It's dry and dead the moment it is born,
     And if it lives a day
It is accounted as a hundred years.)

The poet also achieved some of his greatest successes in serious lyricism, for instance in his well-known *Consolation to M. Du Périer, Gentleman of Aix-en-Provence, on the Death of his Daughter.* However, he is perhaps more at ease in light love poetry and society lyrics. In these he sometimes delights in tilting at the courtly ethos or code in accordance with which the knight abandons himself to a fatal passion while his lady remains aloof and inaccessible. For Malherbe, on the contrary, there is no love without reciprocity, and, even if Helen were to come back from the dead, he affirms 'Unloved by her, I would not seek her love'[28]. The twenty lines on the *Dessein de quitter une Dame qui ne le contentait que de promesses* is a little masterpiece of bantering humour as well as poetry,

Beauté, mon beau souci, de qui l'âme incertaine
A, comme l'Océan, son flux et son reflux,
Pensez de vous résoudre à soulager ma peine,
Ou je me vais résoudre à ne la souffrir plus.[29]

(Fair one, my torment fair, whose wavering heart
Has like the ocean many an ebb and flow,
Make ready to resolve to ease my smart
Or I'll resolve no more to have it so.)

But it is in his official lyrics that Malherbe's finely chiselled work shows to its best advantage and finds its perfect justification. In them the myth of Orpheus comes to life. By the power of the word, of this language of the gods which he has rediscovered, the poet triumphs over death. Kings and grandees turn to him in order to obtain their most passionate desire – to live on perpetually and, since poetic creation is above all an act of will, there was no reason why he should not accept orders for such poems. In this way he becomes a manufacturer of glory and a purveyor of immortality. Malherbe repeatedly dwells on this essential function of poetry, and the adverb *eternally* recurs three or four times with solemn majesty in the key passages of his work. Verse is the only gateway to survival in man's memory, he declares to King Henri IV in 1606:

> Par les Muses seulement
> L'homme est exempt de la Parque
> Et ce qui porte leur marque
> Demeure éternellement . . .

> (Only by the Muses' power
> Can man avoid death's bark,
> And all things bearing their mark
> To eternity shall flower) . . .

It was a rare piece of good fortune for the King to have a genuine poet at hand. Malherbe does not scruple to drive the point home:

> Mais qu'en de si beaux faits vous m'ayez pour témoin,
> Connaissez-le, mon Roi, c'est le comble du soin
> Que de vous obliger ont eu les Destinées . . .

> (But that in such great feats I witness you,
> Learn, O my King, this is the crowning boon
> Shown to you by the kindly Destinies) . . .

And he ends the *Sonnet* (1624) by this haughty alexandrine,

Detail from an engraving after Luiken on the
assassination of Henri IV. The popular character
of this Dutch engraving indicates the
widespread feeling aroused by the murder.
Malherbe was certainly inspired by the national
sorrow when he wrote the *Vers funèbres* in 1610.

When La Fontaine's Fables first appeared in 1668, they were an immediate success. This engraving by Chauveau is for the second Fable 'The Crow and the Fox'. This first collected edition appeared fully illustrated, which, considering the methods of reproduction at that time, must have been very expensive.

Ce que Malherbe écrit dure éternellement.

(What Malherbe writes shall last eternally.)

Thus the qualities of compactness and coherence of this ruthlessly polished and re-polished poetry are naturally devoted to the achievement of victory over time.

An empty victory, it may be said. Why should bought praises be given such a magnificent passage to eternity? How degrading for this proud art to be reduced to the level of occasional verse! The facts are different. Most of the events celebrated by Malherbe – the capture of Marseilles in 1596, the assassination of Henri IV in 1610 and the operations against the Huguenot rebels at La Rochelle in 1627 – were of major political importance. This court poetry therefore strikes a predominantly historical and national note. The lyrics which extol the King express the passionate loyalty and love felt by Frenchmen for the person of the King who at the time stood for France and the nation. Thus as it happens, by making it an indispensable adjunct to the glory of the monarchy, Malherbe demonstrates the inherent grandeur of poetry. Rarely has anyone conferred so much nobility on the calling of poetry as this man who compared the poet to a skittles player. A game perhaps, but a divine game played with carefully chosen words which charm animals, move stones and triumph over time. True, Malherbe lent his authority in the following two centuries to a dangerously facile mythological diction, and for almost three centuries he tied French poetry to the chariot of eloquence. But it is a pity that his intellectual and aesthetic lesson of clarity, purity and taut composition has now been lost. Valéry is one of the last to have understood his message. Rimbaud, who is the anti-Malherbe, has carried the day.

FABLE SECONDE.

Le Corbeau & le Renard.

La Fontaine

La Fontaine[30] has a dual, indeed a contradictory reputation. On the one hand, he is frequently written off as merely a poet for children. Generations of schoolboys have been compelled to learn his *Fables* by heart. And he himself seems to have confessed to a pedagogical vocation when, in 1668, he was unwise enough (though there was method in his imprudence) to dedicate his first collection to the Dauphin (the heir to the French throne), then just over seven years old. He was guilty of a further lapse in 1694 when he dedicated his last *Fables,* which were to form Book XII, to the Duke of Burgundy, Louis XIV's grandson, then aged twelve. The fable, if these indications are any guide, is only for the very young. But La Fontaine was careful to add, 'These childish trappings conceal a hard core of vital truths'[31]. In short, La Fontaine maintained that these short sketches of talking animals were not only amusing but also instructive. They provided a course of morals without tears. And yet lovers of poetry rate this facile and superficial schoolteacher as one of the most subtle poets that France has ever produced. The explanation of the contradiction is that La Fontaine wrote a good deal besides the *Fables*. And the *Fables* themselves are not at all aimed only at the simple-minded and at schoolboys.

In an age when the poetic genres were firmly ranked in hierarchical order, La Fontaine chose to achieve fame in two of the least esteemed of these – the fable and the tale. As for the other genres, he gave them a tone which is specifically his. *Adonis* (1658–69), a poem of some six hundred lines which sings of the amours of the goddess Venus and the handsome youth, of the glorious chase which was to prove fatal to him as he affronted the gigantic boar, and finally the tears shed for him by Venus on his death. This short epic is less notable for the heroic verses describing the hunt than for the love idyll in the first part and the elegiac lament at the end. Bathed in ancient myths and literature, this poem with its filmy and melodious words conjures up a dreamlike, Poussinesque vision of ideal beauty, of impalpable and absolute perfection. No jarring note, no harsh reality intrudes to hinder the flight of the imagination towards a marvellous, evanescent and sensual world. The intellectual content of the work is simple, even trite and spare. The whole charm lies in the insinuating and sinuous music of the enchanting verse, as when the goddess appears in her beauty to the young huntsman:

> Rien ne manque à Vénus, ni les lis, ni les roses,
> Ni le mélange exquis des plus aimables choses,
> Ni ce charme secret dont l'oeil est enchanté
> Ni la grâce plus belle encor que la beauté.
>
> (Venus lacks nothing, rose nor lily, nor
> The exquisite array of loveliest things,
> Nor secret magic that enchants the eye
> Nor grace, more beautiful than beauty's self.)   (75–8)

The two lovers spend their days in unutterable bliss:

> Jours devenus moments, moments filés de soie,
> Agréables soupirs, pleurs enfants de la joie,
> Voeux, serments et regards, transports, ravissements,
> Mélange dont se fait le bonheur des amants,
> Tout par ce couple heureux fut lors mis en usage.
>
> (Days become moments, moments silken-spun,
> Sighs of delight, tears that are born of joy,
> Vows and soft looks, transports and ecstasies,
> The blend of which love's happiness is made,
> All these sensations were this happy pair's.)   (131–5)

On Adonis' death, Venus addresses the imprudent youth in a moving threnody on love's impotence in the face of time and death which foreshadows the liquid, harmonious lyricism that was to flower a hundred and fifty years later:

> Mon amour n'a donc pu te faire aimer la vie! . . .
> Une éternelle nuit l'oblige à me quitter . . .
> Je demande un moment, et ne puis l'obtenir.
> Noires divinités du ténébreux empire . . .
> Rois des peuples légers, souffrez que mon amant
> De son triste départ me console un moment.
>
> (My love could not inspire you then to live? . . .
> An everlasting night wrests him from me. . . .
> The moment I implore they will not grant.
> Dark powers of the empire of the dead . . .
> Kings of the shades, allow my lover to
> Console me for his sad departure now.)
> (564, 569, 582–3, 585–6)

She then turns to the solitary haunts and grottoes in which their love found refuge. She begs them to give her back Adonis. They are silent, and she resigns herself to the last farewell. The verse at this

'The coach and the fly'. Engraving after Oudry for the 1755-9 edition of the Fables, one of the finest achievements of eighteenth-century French typography and engraving. The travellers are lightly sketched in at the top of the picture and the horses, straining to drag the coach up the hill, dominate the foreground.

point comes very near a sort of *poésie pure* in which diffuseness and the meagreness of the content enable the plangent music of the verse to attain the fullest resonance. In accepting mythological conventions which might seem hackneyed, the poet creates a universe suffused in a musical and melancholy tenderness.

It is a far cry from these delicate modulations to the earthy, familiar banter of the *Tales* and certain *Fables*. The verse *Tales*, with their pronounced Gallic flavour (1665–85), take the reader into a world of joyous ribaldry replete with amorous and comic adventures after the manner of Boccaccio. La Fontaine's genius is astonishingly rich and varied. He also composed a mythological novel in prose with verse interludes – *Les amours de Psyché et de Cupidon* (1669) in which the story, both touching and humorous, of the heroine's adventures alternates surprisingly with the description of the gardens of Versailles which were then being laid out, or the literary discussions of four friends as they strolled in the grounds.

But La Fontaine is first and foremost the author of the *Fables* which came out in three overlapping collections (1668, 1678 and 1694). Since the beginning of time, fables have been a popular genre. There are fables in the Bible, in ancient Greece and Rome (Aesop and Phaedrus), in India (Pilpay) and a host of others. But this exercise – pointing a moral, usually by means of astonishingly human animals – had always been short, dry and colourless, a device for conveying elementary maxims to children and the weaker brethren. It could not really be classed as literature and had never tempted a great writer. Even in 1674, when La Fontaine's collection had been out for some time and had in fact created a new genre, Boileau did not admit it into his select catalogue of literary forms. The fabulist's success may therefore seem paradoxical. In an age when poetry was spread over a specific number of forms codified and arranged in a strict hierarchy, La Fontaine distinguished himself in a field in which, it was thought, poetry had no business. While creating what

LE COCHE ET LA MOUCHE . Fable CXXXIII.

LOURS ET LES DEUX COMPAGNONS, Fable CII.

'The bear and the two companions',
an engraving by Moitte after Oudry
for the 1755-9 edition. Oudry's mastery
is demonstrated in the foreshortening
of the figure on the ground and the
beautifully natural attitude of the bear.

55

is really a new genre in French literature, he himself takes the line
that he is nothing but a translator and an adapter. He calls his book
Fables choisies et mises en vers. All he has done, he writes in his dedication to the Dauphin, is to clothe Aesop's moral sayings in 'the garb
of poetry'. He was later to admit to no hesitation in borrowing from
the Ancients 'the idea, the figures of speech, and the laws'[32]. The
transposition of the material into verse is referred to as if it were
merely a new presentation of ideas borrowed from his predecessors.
But the fact is that these ideas are utterly trite, that the fables he
imitates as often as not form part of the common stock of popular
wisdom handed down from time immemorial and that his predecessors are not genuine poets. Never has there been a more striking
justification of Malherbe's theory that poetic creation is primarily a
matter of language, the turn of phrase, the fitting together of words
and syllables. It is profoundly true, of the *Fables* as of *Adonis,* that
the substance is the form.

And undoubtedly what the reader looks for in the *Fables* is not
a profound philosophy. La Fontaine, as one of his eighteenth-century admirers observed, is the poet 'of everyday life, of homespun
reason, unworried prudence, the advantage of living among equals,
the need which may arise of seeking help from inferiors, moderation,
the retired life, that is what he loves and what he prompts us to
love'[33]. There is nothing poetic about these maxims. If we were to
go to the absurd length of reducing the *Fables* to the ideas expounded
by them, there would be practically nothing attractive left. The
morals conveyed would never earn the writer literary immortality,
be they depressing observations such as 'The strongest's reason
always is the best' or sage advice to the effect that 'The happiest life's
a hidden life'. It is surely not enough to explain the appeal and charm
of the *Fables* when we have established that La Fontaine is rather
pessimistic on the score of social relations and that his views in this
respect are often realistic and even cynical, that he attached more

weight to personal relations and that he has touching phrases about friendship in particular, or that he does not stand aloof from contemporary philosophic discussions as when, in his descriptions of animals, he comes out against the theory which regarded them as mere machines? Clearly, the moral is no more important for the appreciation of the *Fables* than the legend for the understanding of an engraving illustrating some proverb. 'Tales for tales' sake seems meaningless to me' (VI, 1), the fabulist assures us. But we need not take this statement at its face value. The obligation to conclude with a moral is merely one of the conventions governing the category of tales which La Fontaine calls fables. It is in the tale itself that his real genius is manifest; and it is in the tale that he (and hence his reader) 'takes the utmost pleasure' (VIII, 4).

It is a very special type of tale, however, since the characters are usually animals. And these are not just, as is the case in the traditional fable, a form of shorthand for human weakness – the wolf standing for brute force, the fox for cunning, the ass for stupidity and so on. For La Fontaine portrays them really as animals, and he has a keen eye when observing them. He dashes off such a convincing life-like sketch of them that the fable ceases to be a dry-as-dust exercise and becomes an open air performance. Here is

> Le héron au long bec emmanché d'un long cou
>
> (The long-beaked heron with long-handled neck)   (VIII, 4),

the weasel who is

> La dame au nez pointu
>
> (the sharp-nosed lady)   (VII, 16)

and

> Le bique allant remplir sa traînante mamelle
>   Et paître l'herbe nouvelle.

> (The she-goat off to fill her sagging tits
> And graze the pastures new.) (IV, 15)

All these creatures live unconfined in their natural habitat. The countryside and the woods are metamorphosed into a world of poetry, which is responsive to every sensation, and every vibration. The reed, for example, is usually born

> Sur les humides bords des royaumes du vent,
>
> (On the dank shores of the realm of the winds,)

a quivering, sinuous line which gives a superb rendering of the physical impression of a water- and windscape. Addressing this pliable creature, the oak points out that

> Le moindre vent qui d'aventure
> Fait rider la face de l'eau
> Vous oblige à baisser la tête.
>
> (The slightest wind that blows by chance,
> Ruffling the water's shining face,
> Obliges you to duck your head.) (I, 22)

The skimpy framework of the fable is no longer condemned to convey a boring moral in abstract terms, but is given flesh and blood, and its dimensions expand till it takes in the whole universe,

> Que tout ce qui respire
> S'en vienne comparaître aux pieds de ma grandeur,
>
> (May all that lives and breathes
> Appear and kneel before my majesty,) (I, 17)

exclaims Jupiter in verses that rise in a cosmic swell. Every line is permeated with an exact and subtle sensitiveness, which breathes life into the form and captures the perfume of the particular scene. Delight in life explodes in and around beings and things in a sort of happy existentialism. Narrow didacticism gives way to the free play of the poetic impulse.

As the fable is neither recognised nor regimented, its telling is left to the poet's fantasy. His penchant for diversity, to which he so often reverts, his art of varying his tone which is the essence of his genius, can therefore be indulged to the full. In the fable called *Against those who are hard to please* (II, 1), he takes delight in parodying first the epic style and then the eclogue. Thus, there is an epic period of thirteen grandiose and reverberating lines:

> Aprés dix ans de guerre autour de leurs murailles

> (After ten years of war around their walls)

and then a charming sample of pastoral style:

> Tircis, qui l'aperçut, se glisse entre les saules.

> (Tirsis, who saw him, slipped away among
> The willows.)

La Fontaine is not even seeking to show that all the genres converge in the fable, for he is not seriously trying to practise them. He refuses to be pinned down by them, and handles them with cool detachment, guying them in fact – as well as his characters, his readers and himself. One of his favourite techniques is to treat a familiar subject in a high falutin' style. The modest heroes, the country animals and people are described in a noble diction as if they were gods, great lords or their apanage. The poet thus creates specifically burlesque effects: A carter becomes

> Le phaëton d'une voiture à foin

> (The charioteer of a waggon of hay)   (VI, 18)

> Un ânier, son sceptre à la main,
> Menait en empereur romain
> Deux coursiers à longues oreilles . . .

> (A donkey boy, sceptre in hand,
> Led, like a Roman emperor,
> Two long-eared coursers . . .) (I, 10)

Two cocks are fighting over a hen; the poet at once thinks of Helen, and exclaims:

> Amour, tu perdis Troie!
>
> (O love, you ruined Troy!) (VII, 13)

But this device is only one factor among many in the continual badinage. The Latin rhetorician Quintilian, he recalls in his 1668 Preface, said 'that you can never go too far in enlivening the narrative'. La Fontaine follows this advice, and the resultant gaiety, he points out, is not 'what creates a burst of laughter, but a certain undefinable charm, a delightful air which can be given to all sorts of themes, even to the most serious ones'.

And in fact the delightfulness of the *Fables* lies in the subtle and varied interplay of a host of heterogeneous factors which all go to make up the total effect – meaning, expression, sound, characters, author and reader. The animals stand for men, but, as we have seen, they are still very much animals. And yet, just as we are looking at the poet's fauna, they are suddenly transformed back into men. Sometimes it is exactly the reverse. We are looking at what seems a transparent symbol for a man, as abstract and emblematic as on a coat of arms, when, hey presto! the symbol fades, and the animal, snapped in an unforgettable pose, is there before our eyes.

The form of expression creates the same kind of uncertainty. It parts company, as we noted, with both the meaning and the characters whom it sets out to depict. In this art of inversion and diversion, this quick-change artistry, there is a mastery which is worth studying in detail in each of the *Fables*. In *The Old Dame and the Two Servants* (V, 6), the dawn of day is heralded in a dazzling and resounding line:

> Dès que Téthys chassait Phébus aux crins dorés.
>
> (Tethys had scarce driven gold-haired Phoebus forth.)

But this splendid daybreak shines on a hideous sight – that of the old woman

> S'affublait d'un jupon crasseux et détestable.
>
> (Accoutred in a foul and filthy skirt.)

There is a never-ending flow of unexpected touches, ingenious ideas and shafts of fantasy that hold the reader to the end. In this creative process, wit and poetry are inseparable, and there is not the slightest straining after effect. We are not allowed a glimpse into the poet's workshop. Hence, this complex and difficult art may give the reader the impression of simplicity, naturalness and even – the supreme triumph of artifice – casualness. His contemporaries appreciated what they called his 'native charm'. One of them recognised in him 'an ingenious simplicity, witty naïveté and an original form of humour'[34]. Another writer calls to mind 'malicious mirth, wanton sport and the elegant Graces', and praises La Fontaine's 'unfeigned playfulness, pure simple naturalness, unadorned, unembellished elegance' and even 'that fine carelessness which in his works often surpasses a more polished style'[35].

Only a flexible and varied versification enables him to achieve such effects. And La Fontaine's skill with his medium is incomparable. He alters the length of the line at will, as his needs and the spirit move him, using irregular verse. This is an instrument which requires the most delicate handling, but which offers infinite rhythmic possibilities, especially when enhanced by the infinitely varied pauses in each line and the carry over of one line into the next. He uses this technique for both verbal and psychological ends – to puncture a gesture, to underline a sudden change, to cause surprise, amusement or a shock. In *The Animals Sick with the Plague* (VII, 1), the lion, who is doing penitence, admits to having 'devoured many a sheep', and adds drily,

> Même il m'est arrivé quelquefois de manger
> Le berger.

> (It even happened that at times I ate
> The shepherd.)

The short line indicating hesitation after the longer one gives an admirable rendering of the comic embarrassment of this confession. Corneille was well aware of the advantages to be derived from free verse: 'The vexations, the moods of irresolution and uneasiness, the gentle reveries, [all this] . . . blends marvellously with the unequal cadences. The pleasant surprise of this unexpected change of rhythm, as it falls on the ear, is powerfully effective in recalling the wandering attention[36].' La Fontaine placed this expressive instrument at the service of his talent as a producer, and made of the *Fables* a drama in miniature. His collection, as he has put it, constitutes

> Une ample comédie à cent actes divers
> Et dont la scène est l'univers.

> (A comedy – a hundred different acts –
> With, as its stage, the boundless universe.)   (v, 1)

A lover of life and movement, a painter, a psychologist, but always a poet, he made the most of all the resources of a nimble mind and all the (invisible) skills of an exquisite art in the minor genre which was his.

3 The seventeenth-century theatre

The seventeenth-century public – whether King and Court or the town (that is, Paris)–was passionately addicted to the theatre[37]. As Corneille puts it in the *Illusion Comique,*

> . . . le théâtre
> Est aujourd'hui l'amour de tous les bons esprits,
> L'entretien de Paris, le souhait des provinces'
> Le divertissement le plus doux de nos princes,
> Les délices du peuple et le plaisir des grands :
> Il tient le premier rang parmi leur passe-temps.

> (. . . the stage
> Is now the darling of all men of taste,
> The talk of Paris, and the provinces'
> Desire, the sweet diversion of our Kings,
> The people's joy, the pleasure of the great,
> For it ranks first among their pastimes now.)   (v, 5)

Performances were relatively infrequent. There were only three companies in Paris. These even so performed only thrice a week, and their repertory was limited. People often went and saw the same works many times. A new play, if at all worth watching, was an event which formed the staple of conversation in cultivated circles for weeks. Objections to this new play were raised by the smart set, by the learned and by other authors. There were replies to these in the *Critique de l'Ecole des Femmes* in 1663. In the same way, an obscure author called Subligny hit on an ingenious way of finding an audience by devoting three whole acts to the *Critique d'Andromaque* in 1668. Plays such as *Le Cid, L'Ecole des Femmes* or *Phèdre* gave rise to a whole critical literature which was sometimes on the weak side but whose very existence was significant.

Corneille, Molière and Racine were therefore able to count on a public which, if it was not always enlightened, was at least avid

Melpomène the tragic Muse, wearing sumptuous theatrical
costume. The crown at her feet indicates the grandeur
of the tragedy. The handkerchief in her hand is to dry the
tears that she will provoke. (Engraving by Bonnard, towards
the end of the seventeenth century.)

Melpomene.

A l'habit de Théâtre que porte cette Muse, au mouchoir qu'elle tient, au poignard,
et a la couronne qui Sont a Ses pieds, on la reconnoist aisément pour l'Inventrice
de la Tragedie, dont Le Sujet roulle ordinairement Sur les malheurs des Grands
Eschyle, Sophocle, Euripide chez les Grecs, ont excellé dans ce genre; Seneque
chez les Romains, et en France, M.ʳ Corneille L'aisne, et M.ʳ Racine.

H Bonnart, ex au Coq, auec priuil

of novelty, attentive and enthusiastic. They were encouraged, pat-
ronised and pensioned by the King and the great nobles. In spite of
an occasional distressing lack of understanding, and of internecine
rivalries, they attained glory in their own lifetime, and in the end
their contemporaries were able to distinguish between them and a
dozen other minor dramatists whose plays they also went to see.
On the other hand, like their fellow authors, they were obliged to
do battle with the religious and moral condemnation which at that
time weighed on the French stage. Corneille, in the preface to *Attila,*
Molière in that to *Tartuffe* and Racine in that to *Phèdre* covered the
same ground, using the same arguments. They affirmed that the
theatre at that time, as was the case with the Ancients, corrected
men's defects and could be considered as a school of virtue. They
themselves were anxious to maintain the dignity of their art, and in
particular they carefully avoided anything that could offend against
decency and propriety. These efforts and precautions did not prevent
the outbreak (in 1694) of a new and serious *Quarrel* over the morality
of the stage; it was marked by the intervention of Bossuet, and at
one point Louis XIV was thinking of closing the theatres.

Drama, both tragic and comic, forms an essential part of poetry as in this illustration. On the left, a performance of *Cinna* (Act V, scene 1) is in progress: the plumed hats and periwigs were still the custom for Roman tragedy and the spectators are seated on the stage. (Engraving by Le Pautre for Perrault's *Le Cabinet des Beaux Arts*, 1690.)

The dramaturgy which is usually referred to as *classical,* with its host of precepts, rules and conventions, gradually secured acceptance between 1630 and 1640. Henceforth the action of a play was expected to have an organic unity, so that the main plot and the sub-plots were closely interlinked. This meant that no incident or episode could take place if it did not have a direct bearing on the unfolding of the plot. In addition, the duration of the play was not to exceed twenty-four hours. It should even be as near as possible to the privileged situation in which time for the characters on the stage coincided with that for the spectators in the audience. 'It would even be desirable', observed the major theorist D'Aubignac, author of the *Pratique du théâtre* (1657), that 'the action in the poem did not call for more time in fact than the time needed in the performance.' (II, 7) Lastly, the whole play had to be acted in the same place. These recommendations constitute the famous rule of the Three Unities which Boileau was to formulate in 1674 in his *Art Poétique* (III, 45–6):

> Qu'en un lieu, qu'en un jour, un seul fait accompli
> Tienne jusqu'à la fin le théâtre rempli.
>
> (In one place, in one day, a single deed complete
> Should hold the stage filled to the very end.)

This rule is only one proposition in the system which also demands a strictly controlled development of the plot – the problem being set out in the exposition, stated in dramatic terms in the crux and resolved in the *dénouement,* i.e. the ending. It also includes the justification of the characters' exits and their entrances, the transposition of acts into words in the narrative speeches *(récits),* etc. Its main aim, it will be clear, was to give the theatrical work an intellectual shape, a psychological and aesthetic framework and a coherent unity. But this system by itself cannot account for either the significance or the quality of the works which conformed to it. Whether they were shallow or profound, mediocre or sublime, there was little resemblance between them, and a play was not regarded as good simply because it observed the unity of time or because the exits and entrances were skilfully contrived.

Moreoever, the two basic genres of tragedy and comedy were not so sharply defined or separated as is sometimes imagined. For a considerable time, a common type of dramatic production was the tragi-comedy – a tragedy with a happy ending. In addition, in a play like Corneille's *Agésilas* which is called a tragedy, the comic elements take pride of place. The tragic genre inspired a wide range of works. Racine's tragedies belong to a different world from those of Corneille. Not only so, but, as we shall see, neither author's works can be reduced to a single type. The same applies even more obviously to the comic genre and Molière. The fact is that, if we penetrate behind the appearances and surface resemblances, the splendid theatre of the seventeenth century represents a miraculously continuous and constantly evolving creative effort.

Corneille's tragedies

As a result of an oversimple and restrictive tradition, it has long been contended that of all Corneille's plays[38] only a handful of tragedies such as *Le Cid, Horace, Cinna* or *Pompée* (1637–43) deserve to survive. By disregarding all the rest, critics have had no trouble in reducing Corneille's genius to a few dramatic devices, some psychological stances and a certain lofty tone, and thus, by an obvious over-simplification, they have frozen the founder of the classical theatre in a pose of exaggerated sublimity. And yet, to take one example, as early as the seventeenth century La Bruyère admired 'the extraordinary variety and the lack of resemblance between the plots of such a large number of dramatic works composed by him' (I, 54). And in fact his thirty-two plays show a prodigious range of

The author of *Le Cid* is shown in this portrait by Le Brun not as a poet or dramatist but as a lawyer (Corneille practised law at Rouen.)

talent. Far from having worked to a formula, the prisoner of a world view or of a dramatic technique, Corneille again and again struck out in original directions, renewing his strength and genius over forty long years of writing. His work pulsates with an extraordinary creative vitality. A tragedy follows a comedy or a tragi-comedy; a tragedy-ballet comes after a heroic comedy; and within the same genre there are profound differences between the plays.

All through his career the poet dwells on this constant self-renewal with a kind of pride. On publishing his second play *Clitandre* in 1632, he harks back to *Mélite,* his first, and observes 'that never perhaps were two plays by the same hand so different both in content and style'. In 1651 he introduces his *Nicomède:* 'This is a rather extraordinary play. It is the twenty-first which I have had performed and, when one has had forty thousand of one's lines delivered, it is really difficult to find something new to say without straying slightly from the highway and running the risk of losing one's bearings.'

Captain Matamore, after Callot.
The boastful and cowardly soldier,
a descendent of the *miles gloriosus*,
is a well-known character in farce.
Corneille used him in his
Illusion Comique.

But he is not frightened by this danger, and he carried on with his soundings. Fifteen years later he was to use the same words to introduce one of his most disconcerting efforts, *Agésilas,* his twenty-eighth play: 'There is, it is true, some risk of losing your way, and indeed you do lose it fairly often when you leave the beaten track; but you do not lose your way every time you stray from it.'

Corneille runs the whole gamut of experimentation in playwriting, and his work offers a fascinating study. With such works as *Mélite, La Galerie du Palais* and *La Place Royale* (1629–34), he created an original type of five-act comedy in verse. The love interest, touched in with light, free strokes, is only a convenient framework. What really charms the audience is the naturalness, the freshness and the grace of the young people in the play, the badinage and the wit, the truth to life of the attitudes, the penetrating observation of the manners of the age – all in a simple, colloquial style which, as he puts it in the *Analysis of Mélite,* reproduces 'the conversation of people of good breeding'. The Paris of Louis XIII, inevitably, is closely worked into a plot which is rooted in everyday life. People meet in the Place Royale or in the arcades of the law courts in front of the draper's or bookseller's, and the atmosphere of these localities is all-pervading enough to give the plays their titles. Money is very much to the forefront, and one marriageable young lady makes no bones about letting it be known that she has 'expectations'. The customs of the time keep breaking in. In this topical and unembellished setting, long before Marivaux and Musset, we meet girls who are unaffected but subtle, who have a feeling heart but an ironical turn of mind. They dream of love while the young men courting them launch out on the discovery of themselves and the hunt for happiness. In these works, the laughs are not raised, as they are in the traditional comedy, by actors playing the clown 'such as the farcical servants, the spongers, the swashbuckling soldiers, pedants, etc.' And indeed comedy often plays second fiddle to feeling. 'My

vein', the author explained in 1634, 'is not devoted only to fun and
games and to making people laugh . . . Often it combines the lofty
buskin with the comic sock, and at one and the same time pleases the
audience by striking contrasting notes'[39]. This genre of serious
comedy (and even, before its time, of the middle-class drama – the
drame bourgeois) was to be further developed in the eighteenth
century and to prove highly successful.

But at about the same time as Corneille wrote these three 'contemporary' comedies, he produced in *Clitandre* an Elizabethan play
in which fantasy runs wild. The stage changes from a wood to a
prison, and then to a cave. Before the spectator's eyes, Pymantes
tries to rape Dorisa who in her turn puts out one of his eyes. Frenzied, utterly improbable actions are enacted in an entirely fanciful
world. As for the *Illusion Comique* (1636), that 'strange monster' as
Corneille himself calls it, it has a play within a play, and at times the
swashbuckler, a year before *Le Cid*, seems to foreshadow Rodrigo

whom it parodies crudely in advance:

> Le seul bruit de mon nom renverse les murailles

> (At my mere name the castle's walls collapse)   (II, 2)

Corneille who was subsequently to make such good use of the *récit* – the narrative speech – as an essential ingredient in the classical theatre, announces in the preface to *Clitandre* that he has actually put events on the stage (instead of merely into words). And he adds: 'Whoever is willing to weigh the advantage of action against these long and boring narratives will not be surprised at my preference for diverting the eye to burdening the ear.' Almost twenty years later, after having indeed appealed much more to the mind than to the eye in four or five of the finest tragedies of the seventeenth century and having charmed the ear with so many admirable lines, yet nevertheless he continued to delight and astonish visually. If he composed *Andromède* to exploit the scene-shifting or changing machines which had just been installed in the Théâtre du Petit Bourbon, it was because he believed in what he was doing. 'My main aim in this play', he observes, 'has been to satisfy the visual sense by the gorgeousness and the variety of the scenery and not to appeal to the intellect by cogent arguments or to touch the heart by delicate representations of the passions.'

There is thus no point in trying to impose uniformity on the torrential and varied output of this theatrical Proteus. Does this mean that his inspiration would have been even more unrestrained, that we would have had a French Shakespeare in all his grandeur if the respect for the rules which were beginning to be enforced had not stifled his creative urge? We know the violent thesis put forward in 1827 by Victor Hugo in the preface to his drama *Cromwell*. He contended that virulent and often stupid criticism of *Le Cid* by envious rivals crushed the poet's spirits, and 'it was only after having been hamstrung at his first try that this utterly modern genius, whose

spiritual home was Spain and the Middle Ages, was forced to be false to himself and to plunge into ancient classical antiquity and give us his Castilian Rome, sublime unquestionably, but in which ... we can discover neither the real Rome nor the real Corneille'. A literary myth of this kind must of course be given short shrift. *Don Sanche,* a dozen years after *Le Cid,* is still another Spanish play. As for Greek and Latin antiquity, the author of *Héraclius* and *Pertharite,* which update it to the seventh century, has the knack of finding in it unfamiliar crannies from which he extracts the intricate happenings and surprise effects needed for his plots.

But in fact he has himself left us in no doubt as to where he stood on this point. In the preface to *La Suivante* published in 1637 when the battle over *Le Cid* was at its height, he begins by pointing out that he has already complied with the famous rules: 'There is only one main plot to which all the others are subordinated. The scene does not take up more space than the stage, and the duration is not longer than the time taken to act it, if an exception is made for lunch which falls between the first and second acts. I have even ensured that there is a link between the scenes which is merely an embellishment and not a precept.' He then goes on to define the position which he was always to adopt. 'I like following the rules, but, far from becoming their slave, I relax or tighten them up as my subject demands, and I even make no bones about breaking the rule regarding the duration of the plot when it bears so harshly on the work as to be incompatible with the finer points of the events described. To know the rules is one thing; to possess the secret of taming them adroitly and harnessing them to our stage is a very different one. And, to make a play a success, it is, I suggest, not enough these days merely to have read up Aristotle and Horace.' This conception of the rules was to be put forward by Corneille every time the occasion arose. In 1639 in the preface to *Médée,* his first tragedy, published four years after it was performed, he once again reminds his readers that the aim 'of drama is to please, and the rules laid down for it are only devices to make it easier for the poet to achieve that end, and not reasons to persuade the spectator that something pleases him when he does not really like it'. Stung by the quibbles of the pedants, Molière and Racine were to take the same line. With his ingenious turn of mind and his remarkable inventiveness, Corneille forged the classical theory into a relatively flexible instrument which he used especially when he felt it was in his interest and for the purposes peculiar to his needs.

For him, unity, to take one example, is by no means coterminous with simplicity. He has a predilection for meaty plots and complex actions. In *Le Cid,* Rodrigo himself, in the space of twenty-four hours, is the hero of two duels and a battle with the Moors, not counting the moral debates which cause, or are caused by, these events. In *Othon* (1664) the hero, involved in the sports of ambition and love, is about to marry first Plautina, then Camilla, then Plautina again, then in the end Camilla. After having thus stunned the spectator with these theatrical feats, Corneille proudly observes 'There has not yet been a play in which so many marriages are planned without any being concluded. These are palace intrigues of which one undoes the other.' In an age when the theorists were beginning to demand – not by the way always successfully – credibility, Corneille states his preference for incredible situations which history or tradition, by guaranteeing their authenticity, can induce the spectator to accept. 'The great issues which stir the passions deeply, and provoke impetuous clashes with the laws of duty or the ties of blood,' he observes, 'must always strain our belief.' *(First Discourse).* And in fact this incredible but true type of plot inspires many of his romantic and stirring tragedies in which, as in *Rodogune,* he has often recourse to melodramatic techniques calculated, he writes, 'to produce a degree of agreeable suspense in the listener'.

But, despite his irrepressible originality and, as some writers

Frontispiece for an edition of *Le Cid*.
Chimène and Don Diègue plead their cause before the
king (Act II, scene 8): the daughter of Don Gormas
demands vengeance for her father, Rodrigue's father
offers his own head so that his son's should be spared.
(Engraving by David after Chauveau.)

would put it, his baroque inclination towards an aesthetic of the
grandiose, the surprising and the dynamic, it is Corneille who is the
real creator of the genre later known as *classical tragedy*. If he delights in the incredible, he is always at pains to make characters and
behaviour ring true. The plot in *Othon,* as we have just seen, is
crammed with unexpected developments. None the less, he dwells
on two qualities of his play which might well be regarded as incompatible with a plot of this kind – skill in the handling of the
action and 'sensibleness in reasoning'. The values of logic, tautness
and craftsmanship triumph in most of his tragedies, and their
structure and expert design fill the connoisseurs with admiration.

The play is treated as a dramatic problem. All the data are conveyed to the audience in the first act which 'must contain the seeds
of all subsequent action' *(First Discourse)*. As for the solution, it
is determined by the events themselves as they unfold. These 'must
be so closely interconnected that the final events flow from the pre-
ceding ones'. The solution must appear to be complete and definitive
when the curtain falls. The problem thus solved is above all a
psychological one. It arises from the conflict between types of
character, ideologies, feelings or passions. And, when there are
coups de théâtre, what is important is not these dramatic developments, but their psychological consequences. Thus for the characters language is both a means of expression by which they define
themselves as autonomous beings, and the instrument and the
weapon which they use to influence the others and ensure the triumph
of their plans. Eloquence, then, which plays such a large part in this
theatre, corresponds to both a psychological and a dramatic necessity. The poet, notes Corneille, 'needs rhetoric to portray the passions and the stresses of the mind, to consult, deliberate, exaggerate
or attenuate' – an invisible rhetoric, incidentally, which the spectator should only grasp via its effects. Thus was built up the French
mode of tragedy in which kings and nobles settle their fate in a

matter of hours – and thus bear witness to the state of man – in a sequence of closely interlinked speeches, in accordance with the logic of the situations and the essence of the passions.

The adjective *cornélien* is currently employed in French without direct reference to Corneille to describe an inescapable if painful and sublime choice between two equally fundamental demands. At first sight, these options seem to lie at the heart of some of his best-known tragedies. But in fact this only appears to be so, and these options are fictitious, or in any case they do not have the meaning attributed to them in common parlance. Seen from this angle, most of Corneille's plays are not *cornélien*. In *Le Cid*, for example, Rodrigo is by no means forced, as an oversimplified interpretation would have it, to choose between love which is alleged to be a passion replete with weaknesses and honour which dictates his duty. The carefully pondered love, which one feels for and claims from someone whom one deems worthy of it, is also a duty. Rodrigo goes so far as to affirm in a lyrical meditation at the end of the first act

> Je dois à ma maîtresse aussi bien qu'à mon père.

> (Duty's not only to my mistress. It
> Is also to my father.)

Moreover, the two types of duty do not really conflict. If he does not avenge the insult done to his father, Rodrigo will draw down on himself the contempt of Ximena and will thereby forfeit her love for him, for that love implies esteem and even admiration. Paradoxically it is his love for her, as well as his honour, that forces him to kill his sweetheart's father and thus to raise an obstacle between the two lovers which might to some appear insurmountable. As soon as Rodrigo has transcended the basic option between coward-ice which would have involved the loss of everything – honour and love – and heroism, which is his vocation, he has no alternative but to fulfil his destiny as a hero. In this as in other tragedies, what is *cornélien* is the intolerable and sometimes agonising situation in which the character is trapped and from which he can free himself only by shouldering his responsibility as a hero.

Now as it happens, Corneille's characters are nothing if not heroes. Rodrigo, Horace, Augustus and Nicomèdes are of more than human stature. Endowed with extraordinary moral strength, they possess to the utmost degree the virtue of *générosité* (nobility of soul); they are ready to devote all their inner resources to the task of incarnating their sublime image of themselves. Will-power, self control, courage and judgment, all these enhance man's powers and his greatness. In the humanist world in which they live, it would seem that nothing – misfortune, suffering or catastrophe – can undermine their overweening integrity. Fortified by their energy and stoicism, they have nothing to fear at the hands of Destiny. They will parry its blows, or bear them uncomplainingly. Fate may dog their steps. For them, it is nothing but a congeries of external accidents and mishaps, and it is powerless to force an entry into their hearts and alter their resolve. Man is entirely free and fully responsible. He has no grounds for dreading the gods. When treating the most sombre theme in Greek tragedy, Corneille in his *Oedipe* (1659) radically transforms the spirit of the legend and does not shrink from writing

> Le Ciel, juste à punir, juste à récompenser,
> Pour rendre aux actions leur peine ou leur salaire
> Doit nous offrir son aide, et puis nous laisser faire.

> (The heavens, fair in reward and punishment,
> To give to deeds their penalty or meed
> Must offer us their aid, then let us act.)

This concept of free will is clearly borrowed from the Jesuits and the humanist tradition. The tragic element in Corneille, then, is not to be sought in the pathetic helplessness of the characters but in the harrowing circumstances in which a wicked fate has placed them. What we have, in a way, is a tragedy of circumstances, over which the hero must rise superior, relying on his own forces.

But he does so only after exacting and grievous efforts. Corneille's characters are no cardboard supermen. For them, heroism is not a second nature to which they need merely abandon themselves. They are not sublime automata. They know what suffering is, and they sometimes vent their feelings in lyrical stanzas and in monologues. They are tugged this way and that. They are rent by inner conflicts, and they admit as much. Ximena confesses that Rodrigo 'tears [her] heart to pieces'; but, she adds, it is 'without dividing [her] soul' (III, 3); Pauline also, in *Polyeucte,* recognises that her duty 'tears her soul' although it 'does not alter its resolve' (II, 2). There is no doubt that we must jettison the half-baked concept of the swashbuckling Cornelian hero, always sure of himself and unhesitatingly sublime, whose greatness is manifested primarily in a staggering boastfulness. Even Augustus (in *Cinna*) complains of having 'a wavering heart' (IV, 3). It is only at the end of the play when he proves victorious over himself that he exclaims (and this is more wishful thinking than actual fact):

Je suis maître de moi comme de l'univers

(I am
Lord of myself as of the universe)   (V, 3)

There is a quivering sensitivity at loggerheads with itself, a three-dimensional reality, in these characters who are too readily described as being all of a piece. Heroism is not something already conferred on them. It is conquered stage by stage as the action unfolds. The hero takes shape before the spectator's eyes. People are not born heroes, they become heroes. Corneille's *Theatre* is, in the literal sense of the phrase, 'a school of moral greatness'.

This greatness is not always synonymous with goodness and virtue. A great crime is also a great deed. Moral power and energy are important in their own right and not only because of the enterprises on which they are brought to bear. Thus, Cleopatra's crimes in *Rodogune* (1644) 'are accompanied by a moral greatness which has something so grandiose about it', notes Corneille, 'that, at the same time as we detest her actions, we admire the source from which they spring'. *(First Discourse)*. What one has to do is to arouse in the spectators' hearts a feeling of astonishment, indeed a transport, whether of horror or admiration, at the deeds of which man is capable at the summit of his powers. Now in Corneille the hero arrives at this paroxysm only when the society in which he lives and his place in it are challenged, when his *gloire* – that is, his dignity, his reputation, his honour – are at stake, as well as the safety of the state. Political interests are regarded as providing the hero with the best opportunity and means for their fulfilment. Hence their important role in this theatre. Love, as against this, remains in the background, for tragedy 'calls for some great issue of state . . . and seeks to arouse fears for setbacks which are more serious than the loss of one's mistress'. In *Sertorius* (1662), one character asks

> Lorsqu'on fait des projets d'une telle importance,
> Les intérêts d'amour entrent-ils en balance?

> (When plans of such importance are conceived,
> Can one put in the balance thoughts of love?) (I, 3)

And in the same play, another character gives the following advice:

> Laissons, Seigneur, laissons pour les petites âmes
> Ce commerce rampant de soupirs et de flammes.

> (Let us, my lord, let's leave for petty souls
> This lowly give and take of amorous sighs.) (I, 3)

Love, which is convincingly portrayed in many guises in such a host

First day of the *Divertissements de Versailles.*
The opera *Alceste* by Quinault, with music by
Lully, is performed before the King and Court.
Opera became so fashionable that at one time
it threatened the other theatrical genres.
(Engraving by Le Pautre, 1676.)

of characters, may prove their downfall. It cannot shape their destiny. The tragic factor in Corneille, with its loftiness and pomp, is usually to be found in the hero in the City State, grappling victoriously with the political and historical vocation which his name thrusts upon him.

Molière's comedies

Although a play is written for the stage, Corneille and Racine can be enjoyed in print, and indeed a careful reading may be even more rewarding than a poor performance. This is not always true of Molière[40]. In some of his works, much of the impact is lost if we have recourse to the text alone. He was fundamentally a producer and an actor, a man of the theatre intent above all on putting on a show. Molière never regarded himself as a writer by profession, and he was never particularly keen on seeing his works adorn a library shelf. His earliest comedies appeared in print against his will, and when he died in 1673 seven of his plays had not yet been published. For him, the staging and rendering of a play were of basic importance, and certainly as essential a part of the whole as the text itself. Hence, to give the public only the written word seemed to him to verge on betrayal. In the preface to *Les Précieuses Ridicules* – the first work to be published (in 1660) by Molière himself and then only under compulsion – he leaves the reader in no doubt on this point. 'A great deal of the charm with which this work has been credited', he notes, 'depends on the acting and on the delivery. I was much concerned to prevent it from being stripped of these ornaments, and I felt that the success which the work had obtained on the stage was sufficiently gratifying to justify leaving things as they were.' Molière's plays, it is clear, were composed by the director of a company of actors who had a detailed grasp of the aptitudes of each one of them, by a producer who conceived of theatrical effects,

words and the relevant mime as an organic unity (cf. *L'Impromptu de Versailles,* in which he portrays himself in the act of exercising his trade), and lastly by an actor who himself studied his roles thoroughly and got under the skin of each character.

Moreover, Molière seems bent less on leaving a series of immortal comedies to future generations than on amusing the king. 'The only glory to which I can aspire', he writes in the dedication of *Les Fâcheux,* 'is to delight [him]. That is the limit which I set to my ambition . . . And, in a way, I believe I am of some small service to France if I can contribute to the diversion of its king.' But the royal commands had to be carried out at once. 'Kings like nothing better than prompt obedience . . . They desire pleasures which involve no delay, and the works most speedily improvised are always the ones the most acceptable to them.' Molière was forced to perform one *tour de force* after another. He dashed off his comedies under continual pressure, and the success of these diversions, which was

P. Brissart d.

I. Sauvé f.

LE BOURGEOIS GENTILHÕME

at the end of Act IV. 'The Koran is placed on his back,
which is used as a desk for the mufti who makes a burlesque
invocation.' The farcical aspect of the action is underlined
in this unsubtle engraving after Brissart for
Le Bourgeois Gentilhomme in the *Oeuvres complètes*, 1682.

but for one evening, seemed to have satisfied him. In these circumstances it is only natural that he should not always have had time to worry about whether his plots were convincing or even whether his style was sufficiently polished.

Everything in the royal fêtes of Versailles and Chambord – the majesty of the setting, the lavishness of the costumes, the music and dances, the words whether spoken or sung – combined to form a vast, composite work which evokes such differing forms of creation as the ballet, the pageant, the fairy tale in dramatic form, comedy, and also farce, the concert and the opera. The written text is only one factor among many others in the work as a whole, and not necessarily even the most important one. In the *Gazette de France* of 14 October 1670, which reports the première of *Le Bourgeois Gentilhomme,* the work is described as 'a ballet with six *entrées,* accompanied by a comedy which was prefaced by a marvellous concert, followed by a most delightful musical dialogue, the theatrical setting and all the rest being in the lavish style which is the rule in the diversions of this court'. Thus, what might be regarded as the central element in Molière's work – the text of the comedy – is barely mentioned. What impresses the reporter is rather the dances, the music and the setting.

It certainly did not occur to the author to protest at this way of presenting his play. When in 1666 he published his *L'Amour Médecin,* which had been performed at Versailles the previous year, he emphasised the inadequacy of the printed text and the virtual impossibility of any one who made do with it imagining the dazzling richness of the performance. He reminded his readers that, 'plays are only meant to be acted; and I advise only those people to read this one who have eyes to discover in the written word the whole of its effects when performed . . .'. 'It would be desirable', he went on, 'if this kind of work were always submitted to you with the costumes and setting used when we act for the king . . . The tunes and the

Jodelet in *Les Precieuses Ridicules* (scene XI)
shows Cathos the leg wound which he received
at the siege of Arras: 'Feel the scar'.
This elegant interpretation by Boucher
(engraving by Laurent Cars for the 1734 edition)
is typical of the eighteenth century.

orchestral music of the incomparable Monsieur Lully, mingled with the beauty of the verse and the skill of the dancers, undoubtedly confer on them [i.e. the works] graces which they can dispense with at their peril.' Almost half his plays, in novel and varied combinations and forms, thus have recourse to music and the dance. 'It is a mixture which is new for our theatres,' he had noted as early as 1661 in the preface to *Les Fâcheux,* his first comedy-ballet.

He was to revert on an increasing scale to this type of composite work as the years went by, for it was more and more in demand. Lully, who was in the end to become his rival, secured the triumph of music at court, and, soon after, more specifically of the opera. It is therefore impossible to reduce to the printed text *Les Amants Magnifiques,* the *Comtesse d'Escarbagnas, Le Malade Imaginaire* and a dozen other plays of Molière without impoverishing them, and even in some cases making it impossible to understand them. Until recently, the bad habit prevailed on performing *Le Bourgeois Gentilhomme* with the suppression of almost the whole musical part of the work; by an error in the opposite direction, Louis XIV in his old age had Lully's score played to him without the text. But the essence of the play lies in its literary, musical and theatrical totality. An infallible method of infusing new life into performances of Molière, while sparing oneself the trouble of many a dubious production, would be to perform his plays in their entirety, both text and music, with their *intermezzi,* their dances and their 'diversions'.

However, it should not be forgotten that, at the same time as he was taking part in the complex undertaking of writing shows for the court combining the various arts, Molière was pursuing a specifically literary objective. Comedy then came far behind tragedy in the literary hierarchy. In his *Critique de l'Ecole des Femmes* (1663), Molière stoutly contested this precedence. 'It is much easier', he affirmed, 'to indulge in highflown sentiments, to defy Fortune in verse, to accuse Destiny and hurl insults at the gods than

Inv. et dessiné par F. Boucher.   Gravé par Lau. Cars.

LES PRECIEUSES RIDICULES.

to get underneath the skin of men from their ridiculous side, and to make everyone's defects seem pleasing on the stage.' And, as a corollary, he sought to raise the standing of comedy by giving it the solidity and dignity which it needed. Such an attempt may appear entirely unexpected. Not only was Molière at court committed, as we have seen, to turning out libretti and ballets and to organising diversions of a certain literary level, but he also – and we must insist on this point – continued to compose and act farces, a genre regarded as utterly inferior.

He was, as we know, to obtain through them some of his major successes. It was by various farces and soon after by *Les Précieuses* that he had won recognition on his return to Paris after twelve years of theatrical wanderings in the provinces. Moreover, farces such as *Le Mariage Forcé, L'Amour Médecin* and *Monsieur de Pourceaugnac* formed an integral part of the court performance. Lastly, some of the ballets are shot through with farcical traits. The Turkish burlesque

The expressive force of this lithograph
by Daumier for *Le Malade Imaginaire*
catches Moliere's satirical mood.

89

ceremony in the *Bourgeois Gentilhomme* is a case in point. In fact the spirit of the farce is visible in all Molière's work. Broad comedy and buffoonery are not discarded as being unrefined. Even in the most carefully constructed and elevated comedies, we come across words and gestures which, crude though they be, never fail to set the audience in a roar. In the *L'Ecole de Femmes,* the shattering stupidity of the two servants is hilariously funny even if by no means high comedy. In *Tartuffe,* Orgon, crouched under the table, is hidden throughout the hypocrite's attempts to seduce Elmire, the dupe's wife. As for Monsieur Loyal, the usher, in the same play, Dorine, the servant woman, notes that he 'has a most disloyal air'. Even in the relatively serious *Misanthrope,* the valet, Dubois, introduces a note of farce. Molière was resolved not to sacrifice any note, however loud or undignified, in the wide range of comic effects.

He none the less applied to comedy, in some of his most famous works, the rules of dramatic concentration which had ensured the fortune of the genre of tragedy and which had contributed to the acquisition of its prestige. The principle underlying this dramaturgy was that the action should treat the problem simply and coherently, and generally speaking nullify a decision which had just given rise to the crisis. Arnolphe wishes to marry Agnes 'before tomorrow ends'. Will he succeed in the plan which he has devised and put into effect in order to avoid being cuckolded? Tartuffe wishes to put the last touch to his scheme by marrying Marianne and seducing Elmire. Will he achieve his ends? Alceste is bent on making Célimène change her way of life. Will he be able to do so? The interest, that is, does not depend on external events, or on actual incidents or *coups de théâtre,* but on the study and development of character, on the conflict of feelings and ideas and on the moral issue raised. The plot is only of minor importance. In particular, the *dénouement* often falls back on wildly improbable quirks of fate. Such seeming flaws are merely the framework of the psychological picture which the author wishes to paint and which constitutes his only objective. The real action, as is inevitable in these circumstances, takes place almost entirely in speeches and arguments. There are half a dozen monologues by Arnolphe in *L'Ecole des Femmes* which together with the asides, make up almost a tenth of the play. It is language, then, which expresses or at least reveals most clearly and directly the inner reality of the men and women on the stage. Thus comedy, by its concentration on psychology, its virtues of unity, continuity and streamlined tautness, becomes at one and the same time an intellectual construction and a work of art which can hold its own with the regular classical tragedy.

And, if Molière confers on this genre, to a far greater degree than any of his predecessors, the human depth and the literary dignity which it had often lacked, his achievement is not confined to the fully developed and as it were doctrinally pure five-act play in verse. The same qualities of psychological penetration and dramatic presentation are to be met with in varying degrees in the whole range of works stretching from prose one-acters to the other extreme of five-act plays, passing through (among others) the intermediate types of three-acters in verse and five-acters in prose. The playwright does not in the slightest make a fetish of rules which he regards not as the essential ingredients of a mysterious and absurd liturgy, but as well-tried means which tradition suggests as suitable instruments to the creative writer, 'These are only', he explains in the *Critique de l'Ecole des Femmes*, 'some broad, flexible observations formulated by good sense on what can take away the pleasure in this sort of poem.' With an astounding freedom and elasticity, Molière effected the diversification of forms of comedy, unerringly choosing the appropriate one for his public (whether court or town) and his aim as the occasion demanded.

For, while making his audience laugh, he sets out, in a number of plays, to convey certain basic truths, either through his *raisonneurs* (who develop the ideas explicitly), or, even more effectively, by the action itself. He is neither a brainless author out to amuse at any cost nor a philosopher who chooses to expound his views on the stage. And it is as serious an error to neglect his teaching as to underestimate his genius as a comic writer. After all, there is nothing to prevent a playwright from having ideas. The author of *Tartuffe* and of *Le Misanthrope* laid great store by his views, and the obsessive recurrence of some of them is obviously significant. Sganarelle in *L'Ecole des Maris,* Arnolphe in *L'Ecole des Femmes,* and perhaps Alceste in *Le Misanthrope* as well, refuse to grant freedom and independence to the woman they love. They are bent, in a way, on owning her, or, in the case of Alceste, at least on dominating her. But she eludes their grasp despite their precautions and pressures, for nature will not be brow-beaten and a human being cannot be put under lock and key or withdrawn from circulation like an object placed in safe keeping. Isabelle secures her liberty by outwitting her tyrant. Agnes, deliberately kept in ignorance by her odious guardian, is thereby ironically enough prevented from feeling the slightest hesitation about abandoning herself to Horace's protection, and her untutored good sense puts to rout Arnolphe's egoistic arguments and morality. Célimène refuses to give up her social life and to follow Alceste to his misanthropic desert. One must have confidence in women, says Molière, allow them any proper diversion they may desire and leave them responsibility for their conduct. Conversely, women merely cover themselves with ridicule when they turn *précieuses* and adopt affected and stupid manners, or aspire to become *savantes* (bluestockings) and are no longer content to have 'des clartés de tout' (an all-round grasp of things) but give themselves over to confused or ill-digested speculations and deny their natural vocation.

With his feet firmly planted on the ground, Molière shows little or no interest in the supernatural, asceticism, heroism or saintliness.

But he is always ready to spring to the defence of specifically human values. 'Religion', writes (in 1667) one of the commentators who had the best grasp of Molière's thought, 'is only the perfection of reason'[41]. In *Tartuffe* and *Dom Juan* he attacks hypocrisy in religion, the ravages of which were extensive at a time when church and faith had great temporal influence. He takes on medicine too, which, under a cloak of pretentious dogmatism, tried to cover up the absurdity of its techniques and its sheer inability to cure. And of course he makes fun of the vices and failings which have always been the stock targets of comedy – avarice, the ambition to climb into the aristocracy, excessive pride of rank, lightheartedness, tactlessness, an obsession with imaginary illness, and so on. But, if all these defects were ridiculous, the determination to force people to improve, and to introduce aggressive sincerity at all costs, is equally so. Man must put up with his fellow creatures, and Alceste is comic because, having failed to reform them, he refuses to live with them.

However, Molière never goes to the length of writing a *pièce à thèse,* a play written explicitly in support of a particular idea. Indeed, the message of his comic works is not always obvious, for instance, when laughter no longer performs its traditional function of spotlighting defects, holding them up to ridicule and thus trying to reform conduct. In *Tartuffe,* for example, we laugh not so much at the hypocrite but rather at Orgon his dupe. Does that mean that we can be hypocrites with impunity, but should be on our guard against the wiles of a Tartuffe? As for the characters in Molière's plays, so far are they from being personifications of abstract ideas that, three centuries after their creation, argument still rages as to the real meaning of quite a few of them. There are undoubtedly ideas in these works, but they are personified in all their human complexity and indeed in their contradictions. Man is always more important than concepts for Molière. This theatre, in which crude farce bulks so large, is also full of finely shaded distinctions. No one else has perhaps gone so far in reconstructing psychological reality in its endless and many-faceted richness. The characters in Molière's plays are so life-like and three-dimensional that certain critics have forgotten that they are comic; but they are utterly convincing, and, just as in real life, some of the aspects of their real nature always seem to elude one's grasp. And no doubt that is why we will never stop arguing about the correct interpretation. Alceste is often ridiculous, but he also earns our esteem and affection. Arnolphe is odious, but he has also his good side. As Molière points out, speaking through Dorante in the *Critique de l'Ecole des Femmes,* 'It is not impossible for someone to be ridiculous in some things and a gentleman in others'. Molière's theatre in its boundless variety represents a possibly unique balance between strength and subtlety, the delight in visual representation and in psychological analysis, laughter and reflection, the ethical and the aesthetic.

Racine's tragedies

Corneille and Molière devoted their lives to the theatre. But not so Racine[42]. It was only for thirteen years out of sixty (1639–99) that the author of *Andromaque* and *Phèdre* wrote for the stage – from 1664 to 1677. While he never completely lost interest in the fate of his plays, the rest of his life was given over to literary genres unconnected with the theatre – history in particular – and he pursued his career at court. Paradoxically, Louis XIV's esteem for him as a writer led to the proposal in 1677 that he should compose the history of the monarch's reign. It was of course understood that there could be nothing in common between the dubious trade of a playwright and the glorious occupation of royal historian. From then on, Racine became primarily a courtier. If in the years from 1689 to 1691 he seemed to revert to the theatre, it was not to the profane theatre. It was to write the two sacred tragedies, *Esther* and *Athalie,* which

In this lively night-time scene from *Les Plaideurs*
(Act I, scene 4) the judge Perrin Dandin,
carrying bags of lawsuit documents,
is being dragged home to be put forcibly
to bed. (Engraving by Prévost after Taunai
for the Didot edition of 1801.)

were a command from the all-powerful Madame de Maintenon for
the girls whose education she supervised in the convent of Saint-Cyr.
What is more, these plays with their musical interludes and their
pious complexion were written at a time when Louis XIV doted on
the opera and when the court went in for religion, and are at least
as much the work of a courtier as that of a poet.

In the course of a relatively brief career as a dramatist, he produced only eleven tragedies in addition to a comedy called *Les
Plaideurs* (1668). It is therefore tempting to conclude that there is
a greater degree of unity in his theatre than, for example, in the thirty-
two plays composed by Corneille in over forty years of writing. But
that is an illusion. Racine's plays undoubtedly belong to a more
clearly defined and focused genre than the plays of the author of
Clitandre and *Agésilas,* but they are nevertheless extremely different
one from the other. Nothing is more dangerous than to force them
into a homogeneous mould and to reduce them to a single psychological or dramatic type. No doubt we can discern the lineaments of
a certain Racinian technique in his rejections, choices and postulates.
On a more ambitious plane, we can doubtless also sense a tonality,
a colour and a perfume which we recognise as specifically Racine's.
But it is essential to approach each of his tragedies as a world in
itself and to avoid one tragedy contaminating the rest. There is no
progress between them in time; there is not even any continuity, but
a gap between one universe and another. After *Andromaque* (1667),
a tragedy of ill-starred love drawn from the Greek legend, comes
Britannicus (1669), in which the psychology has its roots in Roman
history. *Bajazet* (1672), the tragedy with the greatest bloodshed and
the most intricate plot, follows *Bérénice* (1670) with only three
(virtually two) main characters and with no external action and
violence. Then come *Iphigénie* (1674), which a contemporary saw
as an example of a tragedy without a love interest, and *Phèdre*
(1677), perhaps the greatest love tragedy in French literature. In a

different vein, there are *Esther* and *Athalie*, two plays which have little in common but their biblical inspiration. In short, Racine's theatre shows an extraordinary degree of variety. In his creative writing for the stage his main characteristic is his versatility, his ability to adapt the means to the end, the language to the subject. His attitude towards his material is one of complete self-effacement. As a result, the literary edifices which he erects are clearly distinguishable from each other, and, as it were, alien to each other. No doubt there is a certain kinship between them, but this becomes almost imperceptible as soon as one looks beneath the surface similarities.

This flexibility allows him, unlike Corneille, to evolve easily and naturally in the world of the classical rules for the theatre. He does not accept them as constraints which, if need be, can be forgotten or tampered with, but for what they really are, that is, the indispensable tools of a dramaturgy which is peculiarly his. The subjects chosen by him lend themselves, so to speak functionally, to the application of the rules and even seem to call for them. By contrast, in Corneille the situations are generally complex and at times somewhat tangled in view of the multiple actions constituting them. With Racine the situations are, if not always simple, at least immediately intelligible as a unified whole. In his preface to *Bérénice,* Racine vigorously stresses this characteristic of his dramaturgy of the rules which for him is of central importance: 'The essence of inventive capacity consists in making something out of nothing;' and he adds, with a dig at Corneille who was to remain his most dangerous rival, 'All this accumulation of incidents has always been the refuge of poets who did not feel that they had enough imaginativeness or enough vigour to hold their spectators' attention for five acts backed by the violence of the passions, the beauty of the feelings and the elegance of the language'. As early as his preface to *Alexandre,* his second tragedy (1665), he congratulated himself on writing an arresting play 'composed of few incidents and slender material'.

The simplicity of a play such as *Bérénice* is obvious enough. The whole action amounts to the effort of the emperor Titus to put into effect his decision to part from Bérénice whom he loves, and who returns his passion. And it is not surprising that the action, involving as it does basically only these two characters, can and must come to a head in the space of only a few hours. *Andromaque* and *Bajazet* are certainly not so simple, nor can it be said that their action is laden with only a slight amount of material, but the spectator has no difficulty in disentangling the various strands of the drama which go to make up the subject: the organic unity of the action is no less striking. In *Andromaque,* the four main characters are firmly linked to each other by the tragic chain of their incompatible passions, and every move by each of the four has a clear and foreseeable impact on the fate of the other three. In *Bajazet* Roxana is dependent on Bajazet, since she is in love with him, but he is no less dependent on her, since he is her prisoner and she, as Sultana, has power of life and death over him. Thus in each of the tragedies a constellation of forces and appetites immediately sets the stage, and the plot, by a vigorous interlinking of moves, reactions and counter-reactions, develops its explosive potential. Never has the dramatic theorem been so luminously formulated or demonstrated.

His plays carry concentration to the extreme limit. Everything that is not essential is ruthlessly eliminated, 'The finest scenes', we read in the preface to *Mithridate* (1673), 'are in danger of flagging the moment they can be detached from the action.' This action begins immediately after the event which gives rise to it and which is to precipitate it towards the final catastrophe. The process can be seen, to take a few examples, in *Andromaque, Britannicus* and *Bajazet*. In the first of these plays, Orestes arrives in Epirus and summons Pyrrhus to deliver up to the Greeks Astyanax, son of Hector and Andromache. Pyrrhus is thus condemned to make a choice between Hermione, the fiancée sent to him by the Greeks some time back,

F. Chauveau in et fecit

BRITANNICVS.

Frontispiece by Chauveau for the 1675
edition of *Britannicus* showing the dramatic
banquet scene where Britannicus is poisoned.
The murder is described in the play (Act V,
scene 5), but not actually shown on stage.

99

who loves him but whose love is unrequited, and Andromache, his
Trojan captive, whom he loves but who does not repay his passion.
He for his part condemns Andromache to choose immediately between her son's life and her fidelity to her dead husband. In *Britannicus*, Nero has come to the fearful moment at which he decides to
achieve his absurd purpose. He has just had June, Britannicus'
fiancée, kidnapped in the dead of night. He refuses to let any obstacle stand in his way, be it Agrippina, his mother, or Britannicus,
his half-brother. The monster known to history has been born, and
even at this stage the threat which he suspends over the world is
terrifying. The plot to free Bajazet (in the play of that name) and
win supreme power for him seems on the point of succeeding. But
Roxana demands a final assurance – a promise of marriage. She
says of him

> Bajazet touche presque au trône des sultans:
> Il ne faut plus qu'un pas. Mais c'est où je l'attends.

> (The sultan's throne's almost within his grasp;
> One final step, but I await him there.)   (I, 3)

The whole tragedy lies in the hands' breadth that separates him from
power, but this is an obstacle that he will never cross. Racine's plays
have been compared to a time-bomb with its clockwork visible and
its operation perfectly intelligible and which, once the safety catch
is unhooked in the first act, will infallibly explode in the succeeding
four. The sense of direction in the handling of the action – which,
among other things, calls for a necessary 'interlinking of the scenes'
(first preface to *Alexandre*) – must be grasped by the spectator, and
be recognised and endorsed by him. At the very least, he must never,
from the outset, be tempted to question its inner logic. In other
words, in contrast to Corneille with his demand for the incredible
which really happened, Racine takes his stand on credibility. 'Only
the credible touches us in tragedy', he wrote in the preface to

Bérénice. This precondition must be strictly observed, and, in particular, the historical approach of the plot must be such that the audience can accept it effortlessly and not be 'shocked into disbelief.' Racine comes down in favour of an action 'advancing by stages to its end, and sustained only by the interests, the feelings and the passions of the characters', (first preface to *Britannicus*). This psychological progression must, again, be felt to be convincing by the spectators. The author refuses to cram his play, as Corneille did, 'with lots of incidents which could not possibly happen in less than a month, with a large number of stage tricks, the more surprising the less probable they are, and a host of declamatory passages in which one would make the characters say the very opposite of what they ought to say'. He therefore denies himself such facile effects as unmotivated surprises and extraordinary events. He has, admittedly, recourse to surprise at times – as at the end of *Andromaque,* when Hermione suddenly operates a violent about turn. She has just pressed Orestes to murder Pyrrhus, and he carries out the order. But, immediately after, Hermione drives him off amidst curses with the furious question

Qui te l'a dit?

(Who told you to?)

But this is only when the change has been prepared psychologically and when the surprise flows from a philosophy of man in which it is dissolved and in the light of which her unexpected conduct appears justified. Racine's art of suspense consists in providing a satisfaction for a vague expectation by an unforeseen means but which *might* in retrospect have been foreseeable. The tragedy thus becomes a coherent structure, the outlines of which can be clearly discerned and which rests on a psychological vulgate essentially credible for everybody.

A number of nineteenth-century critics were so struck by this credibility and by the feeling of *reality* experienced by the spectator that they put the tragedies on a par with the crimes and misdemeanours daily reported in the sensational press. The murder of Pyrrhus by Orestes, according to this view, is merely a *crime passionel*. Nero is a young man of good family who, having come into his inheritance, takes the wrong turning. *Bérénice* is a *drame bourgeois* of a man deserting his sweetheart since he has just risen to such an important position that he has to abandon the humble marriage which he had planned before his elevation. More recently the tendency – somewhat less naïve this time – has been to dwell on the savagery of the situation in Racine. By this canon, *Andromaque* and *Bajazet* are cases of blackmail. Pyrrhus gives Andromache clearly to understand that Astyanax, her son, will be delivered up to the Greeks and perish unless she accepts his hand. Roxana, for her part, without beating about the bush, summons Bajazet to choose between her love and his death. *Iphigénie* is full of revolting bargaining to decide whether an innocent girl is to be barbarously sacrificed. Phaedra allows Hippolytus to meet his doom after slanderously accusing him. The scene in which Nero forces June to make her beloved Britannicus despair is of a harrowing cruelty. And the violence of the action is often matched by that of the language. When Nero's mother reminds him of her precious – and criminal – services, he replies acidly,

> Vous n'aviez sous mon nom travaillé que pour vous.

> (You for yourself have worked under my name.) (IV, 2)

In *Iphigénie,* Agamemnon, cross-questioned by Achilles, retorts brusquely,

> Pourquoi le demander, puisque vous le savez?

> (Why ask me then since you already know?) (IV, 6)

We forget that this challenge forms an alexandrine (in the original).

The cliché of 'the gentle Racine' survived for so long only because the reader overlooked the meaning, lulled by the regular beat of the verse, which – with few exceptions, such as the line just quoted – is unfailingly melodious.

But if Racine's theatre is cruel, it is not because the playwright is copying a cruel reality, whether historical or contemporary. Credibility for him is not the credibility of the anecdote or the attested fact. He fashions his reality, he does not transcribe it. He is not out to give his public a brand of truth undersigned by history or chronicle, but rather the feeling that what is enacted is true. Characters, he reproached Corneille, are made in his plays to say 'the exact opposite of what they ought to say'. Credibility, on the contrary, consists in making them say precisely what the spectator expects them to say in accordance with their nature or situation. The aim then is a psychological coherence which must, as we have seen, command general assent. In short, what is credible is what is acceptable to a specific public and conforms to what is usually called, in the seventeenth-century terminology, the *bienséances (proprieties)*. This public was well aware that what was being performed was a tragedy, and would tolerate in that art form what it would reject as incredible and spurious in a comedy, the more so if the work purported to portray everyday life. Credibility must be seen in the perspective of the laws, formulated or not, of the genre in question. The psychological depth which is commonly admired in Racine is to a large extent an optical illusion. For the depth is not based so much on a study of man or on relation to real life. The depth, or rather the impression of depth, stems from the rigorousness with which Racine deduces behaviour and conduct – including especially aberrations and contradictions – from the current conventions. The characters are only convincing if we can accept this point of departure and the rules of the game. It lies entirely in their three-dimensionality and in the inner logic of their development, even if that logic is sometimes the logic of alienation and madness. But this convincingness is only that of life if life itself is regarded as a tragedy.

This analysis will be confirmed if we look at the mainspring of Racine's theatre – the passion of love. In his works, love is an overpowering and totalitarian feeling which invades every part of the soul and usually takes over from the will. It is faithful to itself, and will never weaken and disappear, nor, *a fortiori,* change its allegiance. It is an integral part of the definition of the character. Indeed, in many cases it is love that constitutes the *raison d'être* of the man or woman in which it dwells and with whom in a way it is consubstantial. If love of this dimension and nature is true to life, this attribute is certainly not based on statistical recurrence. As La Rochefoucauld put it 'Real love is like ghosts. Everybody talks about both, but few have ever seen either.' (76) This kind of love, however, is in the literary tradition. It stems from the courtly ethics of the Middle Ages. The novels of medieval chivalry are full of it from *Amadis* and countless others on, and it is continued in *Astrée* and *La Princesse de Clèves.* Corneille had rejected this *galant,* drawing-room love since he deemed that the mushiness and soft living which it encouraged were not compatible with the heroic dignity of tragedy. Quinault, on the contrary, who wrote tragedies about the same time as Racine, and subsequently libretti for operas, accepts this type of love, but he uses it only as a means of achieving facile and obvious effects of rhetorical pathos. It was left to Racine to treat this convention as, in a way, a working hypothesis, and with a most unconventional approach to draw from it the most pitiless consequences. In Racine love is first and foremost dramatic material. It is the rigorousness with which it is unleashed and its dramatic fertility which gives it such a stamp of reality.

A reality which is eloquent as to the state of man. In fact, this irresistible passion finds itself confronted with unsurmountable obstacles. Either the love felt by one character is not requited, and it is

The last scene of *Athalie*: the coronation of Joas.
In the play Athalie dies in the wings and her body
is not seen on stage, but in this picture the
artist has united the two actions that Racine
kept separate into one grandiose scene. (Engraving by
Girardet after Chaudet for the Didot edition in 1801.)

clear that it never will be in view, as we have seen, of the fixed and in some degree *substantial* nature of love. In the tragedy, no new love is born, and no existing love denies itself: there is not the slightest chance that Hermione will start to love Orestes, or Bajazet Roxana, and this boils down to the existence of a law analogous to a prohibition. Or a couple of lovers cannot belong to each other, for they are hamstrung by political opposition which they have no means of overcoming. Nero pronounces his doom on the mutual passion of Britannicus and June; Roxana comes between Atalida and Bajazet. In order to avoid suffering, or even simply to save his life, the hero must pluck his love out of his heart; but he has not the strength to do so. The tragedy begins at the very moment when the will abdicates and when the character – by that very fact – allows gods and obscure powers to people a universe for which he has ceased to be responsible.

> Je me livre en aveugle au transport qui m'entraîne

> (I follow blindly my impelling love.)   (I, 1)

cries Orestes. Racine converted this in the final version to

> Je me livre en aveugle au destin qui m'entraîne.

> (I follow blindly my impelling fate.)

It is the character's decision to abandon himself to his passion that transforms it into a *fate*. The tragedy of the ancient Greeks and Romans focused on external hazards – such as the murder of Laius, the marriage with Jocasta – which are the unavoidable misfortunes inflicted on a passive, unconscious Oedipus. But it is within them and in the lucid experience of their weakness that Racine's heroes find their fatality. Their misfortune no longer flows from the external circumstances undergone by them – sometimes even without their knowing and the less so understanding them – but from the structure of their being. The tragedy is internal, or if we prefer it is a tragedy

of character. In a kind of algebra, the grip of love seems to denote the sway over man of that decisive part of himself which he is unable to control. And it is this bondage which reveals in effect his tragic destiny. In Corneille's tragedies there was an unceasing search for a tragic tension which was gradually dissolved by a painful but effective effort of the will and the 'sovereign reason'[43] of the *dramatis personae*. In Racine, on the contrary, it is the tragic incapacity of man to achieve what alone could give meaning to his life and give him happiness and salvation that emerges from the action itself.

For the paradox of a tragic action lies at the heart of his theatre. The powerlessness of the characters is not already established as the curtain rises. Far from it. Orestes, Atalida or Agamemnon are just launching out, or have already done so, when the drama starts, on a clearly conceived plan of campaign which has reasonable chances of proving effective and of changing the scheme of things. Atalida is out to dupe Roxana and to secure Bajazet's liberation. And there is a moment in the play when she is not far from succeeding. Agamemnon sends Arcas to intercept his wife and daughter before they reach the Greek camp at Aulis; if the messenger does so, the sacrifice of Iphigenia will be avoided. Orestes follows a particularly skilful plan to win Hermione who has up till then despised his suit. He will demand the surrender of Astyanax and thus force Andromache, the boy's mother, to look for protection to Pyrrhus. That monarch will then dismiss Hermione who will turn to Orestes. And this is exactly what happens. Pyrrhus refuses to give up Astyanax. Hermione allows Orestes to entertain the highest hopes if – as is the case – Pyrrhus abandons her. Hence the spectator has every reason to believe that a campaign so auspiciously initiated will achieve its objective.

But things do not turn out exactly as anticipated. Before she crowns Bajazet, Roxana demands of him that he marry her, to which the prince cannot agree; Clytemnestra and Iphigenia, who have taken a different road to the camp, arrive despite Arcas' efforts to stop them; Pyrrhus, daunted by Andromache's resistance, changes his mind and decides to hand over Astyanax. No matter. These are doubtless reverses, but the hero may be expected to find some way of triumphing over them. However, one scene follows the other, and he still cannot find a way out. Little by little, it is borne in on the spectators that each of the characters, incapable as he is of curbing his passion, is completely possessed by it, and, since the opposing passions are equally powerful and hopelessly incompatible, there is no possible solution. Orestes can go on manoeuvring and intriguing. The initial situation remains unchanged. Hermione goes on being in love with Pyrrhus, who continues to feel nothing for her, and on the contrary continues to be infatuated with Andromache who is equally far from reciprocating. The spectator now realises that this action, which he had initially found convincing, is really only a tale full of sound and fury. The tragic action is one in which the character engages because he still imagines that it will bring him to his goal, whereas the spectator knows that it is a snare and a delusion. This vivid and brutal drama is caught and immobilised in the pathetic ceremony in which 'our brothers, fellow men' ('nos semblables, nos frères', to use Baudelaire's phrase) enact the ritual of human frailty with exemplary intensity, only to sink eventually in the quicksands of the foreseeable catastrophe, under the light of eternity.

This dialectic significance of tragedy is clothed in an admirable and many-faceted poetry from which it cannot be separated. The verse is not, as all too often in the seventeenth century, a badly cut garment which flaps loosely and clumsily round the thought. It *is* the thought, and the distinction between form and substance is even more meaningless here than in other cases. When Bérénice asks Titus, how, when they are parted, they are to bear a situation in which

> Que le jour recommence et que le jour finisse,
> Sans que jamais Titus puisse voir Bérénice,
> Sans que de tout le jour je puisse voir Titus!
>
> (When the day dawns and when the day will end
> Titus will never see his Berenice
> And all day long I'll not set eyes on you!)   (IV, 5)

she is not translating into an empty conventional language just the idea that neither in the morning nor in the evening will the two lovers see each other – which is an obvious platitude. The passage amounts to much more than that. It is the lyrical expression, in echoing, elegiac verse, of the pangs of separation, multiplied to infinity by the days to come. Poetry, as exemplified by these few lines, is a language which *signifies,* as its vocation demands, more than the intellectual meaning.

Far from being confined to a decorative role, that is to *the elegance of the diction* (preface to *Bérénice),* it blends with the dynamic movement of the tragedy, on which at certain choice moments it confers an infinite resonance of a different order. The famous speech in which Mithridates expounds to his astonished sons his grandiose plan to carry the war up to the gates of Rome itself gives the character an epic dimension:

> Nous verrons notre camp grossir à chaque pas.
>
> (We'll see our camp swelling at every step.)   (III, 1)

The description of Vespasian's apotheosis gives the enamoured Berenice the chance to celebrate Titus' apotheosis

> De cette nuit, Phénice, as-tu vu la splendeur?
>
> (The splendour of that night did you behold?)

The evocation of that ceremony leads to a veritable lyrical explosion which lends the unfolding tragedy its full pathos and substance. In the same way, in *Bajazet* the image is never merely picturesque or unmotivated. Roxana's words, with their vast implications

> Et moi, vous le savez, je tiens sous ma puissance
> Cette foule de chefs, d'esclaves, de muets,
> Peuple que dans ses murs renferme ce palais . . .
>
> (And I, as well you know, hold in my power
> This multitude of leaders, slaves and mutes,
> All, all enclosed within these palace walls . . .)   (II, 1)

are not intended to satisfy some vague penchant for local colour, but to depict the disturbing power of the Sultana, the tragic efficacity of which is shortly to be demonstrated. A splendid line such as

> Et jusqu'au pied des murs que la mer vient laver
>
> (And even to these walls lapped by the sea)   (V, 11)

abruptly conjures up a vista of boundless expanses, coming appropriately at the end of a tragedy of claustration. And a host of other examples spring readily to mind.

In what seems a uniquely successful undertaking, Racine has built up his tragedies into a polyphonic structure. Drama, music and ideas blend, balance and respond to each other and merge in a delightful and powerful harmony. Phaedra's declaration to Hippolytus (II, 5) is simultaneously the dramatic gambit of a woman using magic in the service of love, a superb passage of musical lyricism, and a pathetic and tragically purposeless effusion. And of course, art and thought collaborate so closely in achieving the overall effect that it becomes impossible to distinguish their individual contributions. Racine is probably the greatest poet of the seventeenth century. He is also the greatest playwright and the one with the most profound (implied) philosophy of tragedy. The miracle is that he should have been all that at one and the same time.

4 The seventeenth-century novel

There was a vast public of novel addicts in the seventeenth century[44], but many of these were ashamed of their craving. A drawing-room genre devoted to a conventional type of *galant romance* and intended mainly for ladies, the novel occupied the lowest rung in the literary hierarchy. In general the learned despised it as a form of light literature, a sub-literature so to speak. The 'novel-maker'[45] was not therefore highly esteemed. Even the readers who devoured these works instalment by instalment did not usually bother to keep them in their library. Complete copies of La Calprenède's *Cléopâtre,* for example, are much scarcer than books such as Father Caussin's *Cour Sainte.* It is clear that nobody took them very seriously.

Yet they met very definite needs, both as regards language and composition and ethics and psychology. All these novels strike an uninformed reader of our time as very much alike, although there is really a considerable difference between them, and he would complain of their being monotonous. A friend of Madame de La Fayette defined them as 'fictions dealing with amatory adventures'[46]. In fact, almost all of them take place in an aristocratic and political world of kings and great lords, and have as their subject chivalrous love, as devoted and constant as it is respectful. 'It is a most glorious thing', observes a novelist of the age, 'to portray an invincible love which dreads neither heaven nor earth, and is even fortified by obstacles and would not be put out if the whole world crumbled around it'[47]. Since the action turns on this exemplary and immutable feeling, the novel obviously stands in need of a rich supply of unforeseen events – rivalries, combats, misunderstandings, mistaken identities, plots, shipwrecks, abductions and so on which will again and again drive the lovers apart. And the novelist is free as fancy takes him to think up an endless string of such obstacles in order to turn out the desired number of volumes before the sweethearts are finally reunited. 'I have seen people', observes Furetière wittily at the end of his *Roman Bourgeois*, 'who, to show where they had got to in a story, used to say "I am at the eighth abduction", instead of saying "I have got to volume eight".'

Thus all through ten fat volumes, through thickening plots, feats of heroism and breathtaking adventures, a kind of amatory epic is developed. A romantic universe is built up in which the utter improbability of the story in no way excludes the subtlety of the psychological reflections or fidelity to nature in the delineation of portraits. The background and the plot are pure fantasy, whether we take the pastoral setting of the sophisticated shepherds of *Astrée,* Honoré d'Urfe's famous novel published in the first quarter of the century, the Persia of the *Grand Cyre* which Mlle de Scudéry wrote around 1650, the ancient Rome of Desmarets' *Ariane* (1632–9), or Mlle de Scudéry's *Clélie* (1654–60). But fortunately, by a perpetual and intentional anachronism, contemporary reality keeps breaking in with a true-to-life picture of human relations in the refined society at court and in the salons, and the predilection for *galant* intrigues and adventures of the heart and curiosity about psychological questions – not forgetting occasional allegorical allusions. All these traits give substance to the long and rather empty tales and help to make up for the facile diffuseness of works which it is too easy to dismiss.

The contemporaries themselves had no hesitation in criticising the novel. In opposition to the elegant society novel of the first sixty years of the century, there emerged a satirical type of work which pokes fun at high-flown sentiments and which is not afraid of vulgar or even sordid reality. Charles Sorel's *Francion* (1623–33) is an astonishingly vivid and daring picaresque novel. Scarron's burlesque *Roman Comique* (1651) dwells on the wretched life of a company of actors. As to Furetière's *Roman Bourgeois* (1666), its very title is a challenge. Instead of singing the praises of a sublime princess of impregnable virtue, Furetière portrays a young middle-class girl from the popular Maubert district in Paris who lets herself be seduced. He says at the outset 'I shall relate sincerely and faith-

A character in *Ariane* by Desmarets escapes
from a tower by a sheet used as a parachute.
The artist has rivalled the author in
his treatment of the fantastic. (Engraving
by Bosse after Claude Vignon for Book V.)

fully several stories and amorous adventures that happened to persons who are neither heroes not heroines, who will not muster armies or overthrow kingdoms but who are those worthy people of middling station and who plod along through life quietly and steadily.'

If then the traditional novel is covered with ridicule, this is because its conventions have become thin and are now unbearable. 'What has led people to detest the old-type novels', notes a contemporary, 'is their prodigious length, this mixture of such a host of different stories, the large number of people involved, the excessive mustiness of their subject matter, their unwieldy style and structure and their lack of credibility'[48]. The public clearly no longer responded to imaginary and far-fetched romances, and turned away from the romantic and the marvellous. What fascinated it from 1660 to 1670 was real life adventures or what was purveyed to it as such. As Sorel noted in 1664, 'People were beginning to know what really credible events were through small narrations which were coming into fashion and which were called *short stories*'[49]. To endless accounts of improbable happenings readers preferred true to life and relatively recent sketches recounted without too many preambles. This explains the success of what were then called *histoires véritables* and *nouvelles historiques*. The admirable *Lettres de la Religieuse Portugaise* (1669) were published by Guilleragues, their author, as actual correspondence. The way was prepared for a concise novel, aristocratic like *Clélie* but in a less remote setting, with a more satsifying attention to composition and a far greater emphasis on credibility. This was to be *La Princesse de Clèves*.

The Princess of Clèves

La Princesse de Clèves[50] came out in 1678, a date commonly held to mark the birth of the psychological novel which was destined to have such a brilliant future in France. This is rather an oversimplifi-

cation. Ever since the beginning of the century, the courtly novels in ten volumes had delighted to linger over disquisitions on love and had provided ingenious answers to the questions of conduct debated in the salons. Madame de La Fayette, therefore, with her curiosity as to the problems of the heart and her subtle portrayal of the passions, seems merely to be continuing the genre. In fact she profoundly modified its structure and scope. Instead of reeling off an endless string of rather far-fetched incidents, she described a sharply focused and clearly circumscribed conflict. This explains why the length of her book is kept down and why it is more of a short story than a mammoth novel. Moreover, she replaced the fanciful reveries of a quest for love by the concrete world of reality. *La Princesse de Clèves*, the novel of a married woman, begins at the very point at which this quest ends, i.e. with marriage. From the traditional perspective, which Molière ridiculed in *Les Précieuses Ridicules,* Madame de La Fayette, then, really puts the cart before the horse. Lastly, the work no longer takes place in a highly imaginary Persia or Rome peopled with Arcadian shepherds, but at the court of Henri II, that is, in a recent historical setting against which the author unfolds a drama which is related as if it had actually happened. The interest is therefore no longer in the slightly puerile suspense caused by incredible adventures but in the realistic portrayal of a purely inner problem and its painful solution.

The situation is simple. Madame de Chartres brings her daughter to court and marries her to the Prince de Clèves. But, shortly after her marriage, the Princess meets the Duke de Nemours who falls in love with her, while she, for her part, soon feels for him a passion whose very existence she had not suspected, and which she does not have for her husband. The whole action consists in her increasing awareness of the unhappy situation and her pathetic efforts to escape from it. If she were to give in, we would at once be back in the eternal triangle of the nineteenth-century realists, and the story would fizzle out. But Madame de Clèves was raised on a diet of virtue, a horror of illicit attachments and 'an extreme distrust of herself' (page 18). Moreoever, in the first half of the work, while the plot is building up and the action is developing, four fairly long stories coming at irregular intervals in the form of a digression show the catastrophic consequence of each of the liaisons. These deal first with Diane de Poitiers and the tyranny which she exercises over King Henry II whose ruin she proves to be. Next comes the tale of M. de Sancerre who, when his mistress Madame de Tournon is dying, learns that she has long been deceiving him. Then there is Anne Boleyn and Henry VIII's cruelty to her though he had at first adored her; and lastly the Vidame de Chartres, caught between the Queen and two mistresses in intrigues from which he is unable to extricate himself and which bring about his downfall. The disconnected series of episodes running through the traditional novel are now allotted a precise function. They become stories pointing a moral and are closely linked to the action in much the same way as the chorus in Greek tragedy. Thus schooled by both theory and practice, the Princess de Clèves adopts a brave stance. She is concerned to maintain her *gloire,* that is, her good name, reputation and honour. Her nobility, her dignity, and also her desire to retain her peace of mind, preclude her from becoming involved in affairs in which other women indulge to their ruin.

It is a remark of her mother's which enables her to identify the unknown feelings which she has experienced. 'She had not yet dared admit it to herself ' (page 53). She has no alternative but to accept a passion which she cannot help feeling; but at least she must try not to show it. 'She no longer lulled herself in the hope that she would not love him; her only thought was never to let him see that she did' (page 77). We cannot arouse within us the feeling of love; the Princess 'regards it as a crime not to feel any passion' for her husband, on which the author comments, 'as if that was something

within her power' (page 181). Nor can we suppress this feeling in our heart, but at least we can prevent ourselves from revealing it. Some fifteen years earlier, Madame de La Fayette had noted, in speaking of Chabanes, a character in her first novel (which is really a short story) *La Princesse de Montpensier*: 'if he was not master of his heart, he was master of his actions.' However, this control calls for an unremitting and superhuman effort, of which, as the Princess de Clèves notes despairingly, she is not always capable. 'She found that she was no longer mistress of her words and her expression.' And she is soon forced to recognise: 'I am defeated and overcome by an attachment which sweeps me along despite myself. All my resolutions are in vain. Yesterday, I thought everything that I think today, and today I do just the opposite of what I resolved yesterday' (page 121). All that seems left to her is this lucidity which, as she herself is later to underline, is distressingly ineffective. 'Passions can lead me, but they will never blind me.'

A scene from the life of the royal family
at Versailles. Although the action
of *La Princesse de Clèves* takes place
in the sixteenth century, Madame
de la Fayette often describes court
ceremony as it was in her own time.

The situation is not quite so hopeless, for she can still act indirectly, 'Withdraw from the court', her mother had told her straightaway. 'Force your husband to take you away' (page 56). She now decides to follow this advice. 'I must tear myself away from M. de Nemours. I must go off to the country, however strange my trip may seem. And, if M. de Clèves persists in preventing me, or in knowing why I wish to go, perhaps I shall do him (and myself as well) the ill turn of telling him why' (page 121). As it happens, M. de Clèves cannot agree to his wife escaping from the duties which her rank at court involves. He asks for an explanation, and the Princess, who seeks her husband's support at the same time against herself, is led to confess to him her passion for another – whose name she obviously conceals. With this heroic admission, on which the contemporary psychology disserted copiously, all the agonising possibilities of the situation emerge.

M. de Clèves, who had always been affected by his wife's coldness, is now thrown into a frenzy of grief which rapidly brings him to his grave. 'I have only violent and wavering feelings of which I am not the master', he confides to her. 'I no longer feel myself worthy of you; you no longer seem worthy of me. I adore you; I hate you. I offend you; I implore your pardon. I admire you; I am ashamed of admiring you. In short, every vestige of calm and reason has fled me' (page 162). As for the Princess, not only has she placed an unsurmountable obstacle between herself and her love, as her reason desired, but she has before her eyes the sufferings of a husband whom she esteems and whom she has entangled in the web of her own troubles. As for the Duke de Nemours, he has to be content with the sterile satisfaction of knowing that he is loved. 'She loves me!' he exclaims. 'There is no doubt about that ... Yet I am treated as sternly as if I was hated. I once put my hopes in the passage of time. I have nothing to hope from it now. I see her defend herself equally against me and against herself' (page 170). Husband of the most

virtuous wife that ever was, M. de Clèves dies of jealousy and grief.
Subsequently the Princess is unable to bring herself to belong to the
man whom she considers responsible for her husband's death.
Besides, she retains the same distrust of passion which she had when
that passion was criminal. Time has gone by in vain. The reasons
for her refusal, she says, are 'strong as regards her duty and unsurmountable as regards her peace of mind' (page 198). She will never
marry de Nemours. Like the three main characters in the tragedy of
Bérénice, these three exemplify

> d'exemple à l'univers
> De l'amour la plus tendre et la plus malheureuse
> Dont il puisse garder l'histoire douloureuse.
>
> (The most devoted, tender, ill-starred love
> Whose grievous history time will e'er record.)

The novel, it is true, contains many of the traditional ingredients of
the courtly, society novel. Nemours, as a well-schooled lover, pur-
loins a miniature with the portrait of his lady. A letter which has
gone astray whose addressee is wrongly identified is picked up; this
sets people off on a false track, and it is only some time later that the
error is rectified. De Nemours wanders round the country house
of Colomiers to which the Princess has withdrawn. By a really
miraculous coincidence which in the opinion of a contemporary
smacks of 'the ten-volume romance'[51], he forces his way into the
garden at the very moment when Madame de Clèves is making the
terrible confession to her husband, and he is therefore within earshot
at the time. As to the psychological and moral implications of that
confession, the *Mercure Galant,* a fashionable review – especially
popular in the provincial salons – organised a survey as soon as the
book came out, and one of its readers provided an ironic justification
of the Princess's attitude by observing that 'she would not be the
heroine of a novel if she were not an extraordinary character'[52]. As

it is, Madame de Clèves is herself aware of the heroism of her conduct. 'Ah, Sir,' she says to her husband after her confession, 'there is not another adventure like mine in the whole world; there is no other woman capable of doing what I have done' (page 144).

Indeed, the whole story reveals a romantic penchant for moral prowess, for the rare and the surprising. This is because the characters are out of the ordinary. They are heroes, each one of whom is unique in his own way. But the only trait which they have in common is that they are heroes. M. de Clèves is splendid and noble-hearted as well as wise, M. de Nemours is 'a masterpiece of nature' (page 10). As for Madame de Clèves – and this is one of the few physical indications in the whole of the novel – 'the fairness of her complexion and her blonde hair gave her a glow the like of which was never seen in anyone but her' (page 18). All these exemplary characters live at court in artificial relations which call for a high degree of self-control and discernment. Deep in political and amorous intrigues, they spend their time in a perpetual analysis of themselves and others, and in conversation which is at one and the same time a ceremony, a game and a battle.

But instead of elegant and subtle chatter between witty puppets, Madame de La Fayette offers her reader the moving story of the misfortunes of three people whom she has managed to bring to life. In her novel, the court still stands for a way of life and a level of civilisation, but above all it constitutes a network of obligations which no one is able to evade – Nemours, the Prince and the Princess cannot escape from each other. They are condemned to live together. 'You are my wife. I love you as if you were my mistress, and I see you in love with someone else', exclaims the Prince de Clèves. 'This other man is the most attractive man at court, and he sees you every day; he knows that you love him' (page 161). And it is the Prince himself, it will be remembered, who did not allow his wife to leave the court and go and live in the country as she had wished.

A ball at the court of Henri III by an unknown
artist. Madame de la Fayette describes a similar
scene under Henri II in which the Princesse
de Clèves and the Duc de Nemours meet for
the first time and dance together at the King's
request. Musée de Blois.

Far from distracting and dispersing interest as in the traditional novels, court life heightens the dramatic tension. There is no mystery as to where the novelist found such an effective technique of concentration in the tragedy. Madame de La Fayette saw Racine create all his profane plays up to the last of them – *Phèdre* – in 1677. It is no accident that her novel appeared in 1678 and for the first time provided an admirable prose example of what Racine demanded in tragedy: 'A simple action sustained by the violence of the passions, the beauty of the sentiments and the elegance of the language'. The novel is not even lacking in 'that majestic sadness which constitutes the whole pleasure of tragedy' (preface to *Bérénice*). Madame de Clèves was herself to stress the tragic element in the state of man, the absurdity of the events and the hazards which determine it. 'Why did I not know you only after I became free', she says to de Nemours on the death of the Prince de Clèves, 'or why did I not know you before I was engaged? Why does fate separate us by placing such an invincible obstacle between us?' (page 194).

For the contemporaries themselves, this fine novel at once brought to mind Racine and the tragedy. Writing on the famous confession scene, one of them observes 'Don't you think that this passage of our story would prove very effective on the stage?' And he adds 'What would it be like if clothed in the art and animated by the voice of the actors and sustained by verse such as in *Iphigénie?*'[53] But there is really no need for the help of the actor's voice. Again and again *La Princesse de Clèves* turns into an armchair tragedy. The use of third person in the narrative puts the characters in the current theatrical perspective and turns the reader into a spectator. The action can be split up into scenes – that with the Italian jeweller, that of the meeting of the Princess with M. de Nemours, the scene of the theft of the portrait, the scene of the confession in the pavilion, and so on. And speech follows speech, punctuated by stage instructions which indicate attitudes and gestures; they are grouped in dialogues with veritable tirades, or else in tragic monologues like the one in which Nemours indulges near the little stream at Colomiers. One could easily make a whole study of the dramaturgy of the novel.

But the mainspring of the dramatic unity is, as in Racine's tragedies, the tragic passion which is analysed in all its stages – birth, fulfilment, setbacks, misunderstandings, battles, frenzies, fatal effects. As in *Andromaque* or in *Bajazet,* the whole action consists in an attempt to escape from the initial situation. But in vain. Everyone stays true to himself and the disaster to which he is condemned. Caught in this trap of a destiny which they make their own, the characters take on the majesty of human suffering, and the heroic nobility to which they ascend gives substance to their rather hollow aristocratic dignity. The use of the techniques of tragedy, then, has moral and psychological implications as well as aesthetic ones. The subject matter of the traditional novel, thus concentrated and welded into unity, acquires the three-dimensional richness of life itself. The characters really exist. The analysis is no longer a mere accessory, a brilliant exercise, a commentary. It is action, an action carried forward by each of the Princess's meditations.

Thus there emerges, by a sort of transmutation of the genres, the French tradition of the psychological novel. In giving it from the start its highly integrated structure and its compactness, Madame de La Fayette has laid perhaps even more weight on the qualities of naturalness, restraint and subtly varied realism which are no less indispensable to it. Convinced that art lies in concealing art, and that a good technique should be invisible, she writes *à propos* of her novel 'It is a perfect imitation of the world of the court and of the court way of life. There is nothing romantic or high faluting about it'[54]. A new genre is born in which the element of romance will be absorbed by and hidden behind the *roman* (novel) itself.

Part 2

The Eighteenth Century

La Parade sur les Boulevards by Gabriel
de Saint Aubin showing a type of open-air
miniature theatre which was very popular
in the eighteenth century.

5 The eighteenth-century theatre

The public retained its enthusiasm for the theatre[55] in the eighteenth century; but it was sated with masterpieces and very hard to please, the writers of the time assure us. 'The public', one of them declared in 1718, 'is like a guest nearing the end of a meal . . . When he sat down to table at the beginning of the last century, he made do with the coarsest of fare. Since then, he has been served up the most exquisite dishes and he has gorged himself on them with the keenest relish . . . Even if he were still to be offered the same kind of feast, which is hardly possible, I am not sure that he would react to it'[56]. This much is certain: tragedy, still the noblest and the most appreciated genre, was paralysed by the prevailing veneration for Corneille and Racine – and indeed for the whole epoch of Louis XIV, who was rapidly becoming a legend. The two great classics' puny imitators observed the stereotyped rules, but completely failed to breathe new life into the genre. Classical dramaturgy withered away and degenerated into a ritual. The conventions, instead of underlying a play, now constantly obtruded themselves, for they had no longer any justification. However, writers still turned out a flow of five-act tragedies in verse. But these offered nothing except the standard ingredients – declamations, confidants, unconvincing pathos, laboured versification and the regulation twenty-four hours' action. It all adds up to an anthology of fairish imitations of the most famous passages of Corneille and Racine.

Crébillon, the father of the novelist of that name, developed a special line in monstrous subjects, and turned horror and terror to skilful account. Voltaire, for his part, realised that tragedy must be given wider horizons, and he drew on spectacular effects – history, exoticism, emotion, occasionally trying his hand at the *pièce à thèse* (a play expounding a particular thesis). But, in doing so, he often travestied the spirit of seventeenth-century tragedy, and, what is more, his work did not gain in convincingness.

But at least in one respect there was some progress. The conditions under which plays were performed were modified midway through the century. The seats on the stage itself, which had always been reserved for privileged spectators (to the extreme discomfort of actors and audience), were done away with in 1749 and this removed an irritating obstacle to theatrical illusion. Six years later another reform was introduced along the same lines: actresses were no longer obliged to wear hoop dresses. From then on, their costume was to make a deliberate break with the fashion of the time and to become specifically theatrical. Lastly, in 1782, the pit, where the spectators had to remain standing, was closed.

Comedy was incomparably fresher and more alive. Molière remained the supreme model, and quite a few of the century's comedies are in verse like *L'Ecole des Femmes* or *Le Misanthrope*. But his imitators concentrated on the aspect of his work most congenial to them. In the early years of the century, Regnard concocted amusing plots (*Les Folies Amoureuses*, 1704, and *Le Légataire Universal,* 1708). Psychological comedy now attacked foibles rather than vices. Regnard put on *Le Distrait* (which went back to 1697); Destouches *Le Glorieux* (1732); Piron *La Métromanie* – that is, the mania of composing verse (1738); Gresset *Le Méchant* (1747). The comedy of manners flourished and borrowed from the current scene a new type of character – the financier or speculator, who brought success to Le Sage's *Turcaret* (1709). But the one great creator of the age was Marivaux, who invented a tone and manner which was his and his alone. Some fifty or sixty years later, taking quite a different route, Beaumarchais in his turn broke new ground in comedy.

Repudiating the distinction between the genres, a certain number of playwrights devised a half-way house between tragedy and comedy, with characters who were neither kings nor princes, and aimed mainly at playing on the emotions. In this way arose the *comédie larmoyante* (the tearful comedy) and the *drame bourgeois*

The great actress Mlle Duclos, seen here as
Ariane in the tragedy by Thomas Corneille,
joined the Theatre Français in 1693,
remaining there until 1736. She was
said to excel in pathetic roles. (Engraving
by Desplaces after Largillière, 1714.)

(middle-class drama) so dear to the heart of Diderot. 'Man', observed that writer, 'is not always immersed in sorrow or joy'[57]. This intermediate range characterised what he called the serious genre which was built round professions or *stations* – 'the man of letters, the *philosophe,* the businessman, the judge, the lawyer, the politician, the citizen, the magistrate, the speculator, the great lord, the bailiff', and which dealt with family types – 'the *pater familias,* the husband, the sister, the brothers'. Instead of always falling back on what were (by then) cardboard characters, the theatre thenceforth drew on the realistic aspects of social and domestic life. *Le Père de Famille* and *Le Fils Naturel* by Diderot, *Le Philosophe sans le savoir* by Sedaine (1765) are illustrations (though not very exciting ones) of the new genre.

But the addiction to theatre-going was so intense that it led to the creation of yet more genres. Friends formed small theatrical groups in which they were alternatively actors and spectators. Private theatres became all the rage, and gave rise to a whole repertory, part of which was collected under the title of *Théâtre de société* (Club theatre). It included operettas, comic operas, ribald and at time obscene comedies. It also included *parades,* little comedies written in popular language, often extremely coarse and verging on the farcical. Sparkling and spirited, they went with a swing. Lastly, there were the Proverbs in which Carmontelle[58] made such a hit. These sketches, intended as their name suggests to illustrate a proverb, remain astonishingly natural and close to everyday life.

And so, from the utmost sobriety and spontaneity to the most unbridled fantasy and the most stilted productions, the theatre followed innumerable approaches to its goal – the satisfaction of one of the most deeply embedded needs of the century.

The Italian Comedians depart in 1697, demonstrating their despair in theatrical attitudes. They returned to France on the death of Louis XIV and became the most popular company for performing Marivaux's plays. (Engraving by Jacob after the painting by Watteau which is now lost.)

Marivaux

A novelist and a penetrating moralist, Marivaux is also the author of over thirty prose comedies, composed for the most part between 1720 and 1740[59]. The world in which they take place is a profoundly original one. As early as the eighteenth century itself, the term *marivaudage* had to be invented to denote certain psychological relations and the style in which they are clothed. Before long, the word was carried over from literary situations to real life to indicate attitudes and forms of communication between men and women of which Marivaux has made civilisation aware. He is thus acknowledged to have discovered and explored a whole province of the human heart from which he usually takes the theme and rhythm of his plays. His psychological world is peculiar to him. Hew knew it was, and he wanted it to be so. He stood foursquare in the modern camp, and was opposed to the imitation of the Ancients. On a number of occasions, if we are to believe D'Alembert, he declared 'I would rather be seated humbly on the back bench among the select band of original writers than give myself airs in the front row with a pack of literary apes'[60]. He felt that the role of creative writer was not, as was widely held, to adjust to and perpetuate the traditional examples of a literary genre, but 'to take no one as a model' and simply to be natural, that is, to 'stick to the particular gifts allotted us'[61].

He needed freedom to manoeuvre and the assurance that the acting corresponding to his particular gifts would be forthcoming, and he found both in the actors of the Italian Comedy. Molière's successors had their plays performed at the Comédie Française, but its illustrious heritage of conventions and customs weighed heavily on them. The Italian Comedians, on the contrary, who had been expelled in 1697 by Louis XIV, had just returned to France (in 1716). More flexible, unencumbered by literary constraints, expressive and natural, they were just the troupe to do justice to

Marivaux. Lélio, Arlequin, Flaminia, Mario or Trivelin, and especially Silvia, offered the types which he needed for his plays. There is no doubt that he often had them in mind, with their personal idiosyncracies and casting possibilities, when he was constructing his characters – whom indeed he sometimes called after them. But they never forced him off course, and he preserved his creative liberty while making the fullest use of the resources offered by each of them. In fact, the comedians fitted in with his vision of things much more than they conditioned it. He also, it is fair to add, gave a number of his plays to the French Comedians, and these works do not differ in any fundamental respect from those performed by his favourite actors.

Unlike Molière and his imitators, for whom love is only one component. Marivaux chose love as the theme of most of his comedies. This exclusive emphasis recalls Racine's tragedies in which, right from the outset, passion is clearly the key factor. Marivaux is different, however, to the extent that the tone remains comic despite certain moments of seriousness and even of pathos. And in his plays love is not an absolute passion which is a basic ingredient of the character, but the first stirring of an inclination which is still feeling its way and is often unavowed. It is not the course of love with its problems and misfortunes which unfolds on the stage, but its emergence in a heart that seemed quite unprepared for it, its hesitations and subterfuges. A certain number of his comedies might aptly be called *Surprise de l'amour*, a title which in fact he gave to a couple of them[62]. Other plays deal with the shame-faced resistance to a passion which one character has recognised in his heart but which he is eager not to reveal to the beloved. Almost all the comedies are intent on forcing love out of the wide variety of recesses supplied by the proprieties and by *amour-propre* in which it obstinately tries to hide. The general advance of the action is that of a sort of emotional midwifery which delivers the character of his secret. It leads him on to a confession – to himself and to others – which brings the feeling out into the open and prepares the *dénouement* expected by the audience. This transition from the implicit to the explicit, this *revelation* – in the photographic sense of the term – allows a playwright relatively limited scope, and the evolution of the action may often seem to follow the same curve. Indeed, Marivaux's contemporaries accused him of monotonousness. He rejected the charge, and stressed the host of situations which could be exploited in his special field – the psychology of love. 'My plays', he writes, 'deal sometimes with a feeling of which the couple is unaware, sometimes with one which they realise and wish to conceal from each other, sometimes with a timid passion which dares not speak out, and lastly sometimes with an uncertain and so to speak wavering love, a love, that is, in a way, just coming to birth which they suspect exists without being really sure, and which they scrutinise in their hearts before allowing it to soar'. 'Where', he ends, 'is all this similarity with which people keep reproaching me?'[63]

Sure enough, the variety of this theatre is best appreciated by the spectator who is not taken in by the facile devices carrying the plot forward. For the conventional symmetries, the parallel volte-faces, the reciprocal deceptions, in a word, all the familiar techniques of the standard ballet abound in this theatre with its Italian flexibility and indifference to criticism. In the *Serments Indiscrets* (1732) Damis and Lucile, whom their families wish to marry each other, are set on opposing the plan. In fact they fall in love at first sight but remain captive of their prejudices and of their *amour-propre*. In the *Jeu de l'amour et du hazard* (1730) Silvia and Dorante, who do not yet know each other, but whose marriage has been arranged by their families, secretly and independently decide to masquerade as each others' servants in order the better to size one another up. They start falling in love as soon as they meet. But each is alarmed when his heart is touched not by the one who is taken for the master but by the other who plays the role of the servant, while the same ploy is worked out in counterpoint between the valet and the maid. As one character at the end of *Les Sincères* (1739) observes: 'We have taken a curiously round-about road to get here'. In the face of such a frequent and uninhibited recourse to disguise, mistaken identity, stratagems and in general to the rules of the stage foursome, the spectator often has the feeling that the play meanders along in gently ornamental curves towards an entirely predictable conclusion.

But what we have been discussing is only a framework. The real action is elsewhere. Never in fact has there been such a clear line between plot and action. The action, as a writer of the age observed in a clumsy metaphor, consists of 'the ingenious embroidery' which 'expresses the most hidden recesses of the heart and the most delicate refinements of the mind'[64]. Lucile and Damis are in love by the end of the first act. Is everything over by then and is all the rest mere padding? Not at all. On the contrary, it is only at that point that the real questions begin to emerge. 'Bound as both of them are by the agreement not to marry the other, how will they manage to conceal their love? How will they arrange to let the other know of their feelings? . . . How will they manage simultaneously to keep watch over and frustrate the steps which they must take to avoid marriage? 'This', notes Marivaux, 'is what makes up the whole of the four other acts'[65]. What really counts, then, is the spectacle of a heart arguing with itself, trying to deceive itself, battling with itself or with another heart, its hesitant and contested efforts to achieve lucidity, peace and happiness. In other dramatists, the obstacles to be overcome by love are external. 'In my work', to quote Marivaux again, 'love is at loggerheads only with itself, and it ends up by being happy despite itself'[66]. This theatre is concentrated more than any other on the man (or woman) within. The real milestones in the action are not the pauses in the mechanics which drive it forward, but the successive inner revelations which constitute it. 'Ah! now I see clear into my heart', exclaims Silvia, when Dorante confesses his disguise to her. The playwright's whole effort is therefore bent on bringing about the psychological slow motion in which he is enabled to unveil the true state of his characters' feelings.

The dialogue, with the blending in of the repartee and its invisible transitions, has a continuity and a fluidity which would have been unthinkable in a play in verse governed by the conventions of the genre. With singular skill it manages to be simultaneously significant or even explanatory and natural. For the analysis must be pursued with all the subtlety that is necessary, but in such a way that the character does not lose what is, so to speak, his intellectual innocence. Marivaux does in fact succeed in putting the spectator in a position of superiority over the characters – and this so clearly that they 'never appear to realise the full import of what they are saying, while at the same time the audience does, and can unravel the implications of the words through the kind of cloud in which their speeches have had to be wrapped'[67]. None the less the playwright has been reproached with his metaphysics, his complicated and affected language and his over-witty characters. In reality he has given back to love its moving and undeclamatory reality which a hundred years of largely theatrical love had made people forget. And the vivacious girls in his comedies have a level-headed charm which is hardly to be met with outside Musset. The secret of his success lies in blending, in the wit and affectionate badinage to which he has given his name, so many seemingly contradictory factors – civilisation and spontaneity, intelligence and freshness, intellectual coherence and feeling, analysis and poetry.

Beaumarchais

The author of two dazzling comedies – *Le Barbier de Séville* (1775) and *Le Mariage de Figaro* (1784) – Beaumarchais[68] is an extraordinary figure, as astounding as the main character of these plays. The son of a Paris watchmaker, a watchmaker himself and the inventor of a new system of escapement, a brilliant music-lover who taught the harp to Louis XV's sisters, the friend of a tax-farmer general and early in life a successful business man himself, there was not one talent which he did not possess. Ingenious, seductive, always at ease no matter what the setting and the situation, he had just the type of nimble and resourceful mind, just the devil may care approach and dash with which he endowed his hero Figaro. Sent to Spain in 1764–6 on a financial mission, he was able to take up the case of his sister, who had been engaged to Clavijo, a Spanish man of letters, and then abandoned by him in Madrid. He did not hesitate to intervene forcefully, though he thereby provoked a spate of dramatic incidents. His subsequent account of this episode is so captivating that Goethe made it into a play (*Clavigo,* 1774). On the death of his friend and protector, the tax-farmer general, the heir brought

a lawsuit against him. In the end Beaumarchais lost it because of the hostility of the rapporteur, Goezman. But, on the brink of ruin and dishonour, he counter-attacked in four *Mémoires* (1773–4) which are masterpieces of light, effervescent polemics and in which he poured ridicule on his opponents, thus making opinion swing back on his side. He was then given secret government missions abroad. He also launched into some extremely important naval operations aimed at supplying arms and munitions to the American insurgents, and it is in part thanks to him that they won the battle of Saratoga in 1777. At the same time he turned his attention to the material situation of playwrights who all too often were mulcted of their royalties, and founded the Society of Dramatic Authors. From 1784 on, he published – at Kehl, on the German bank of the Rhine – Voltaire's *Complete Works* in seventy volumes (including some writings still banned in France). He proved equally enterprising under the Revolution. He became embroiled in a deal in-

L'après-dîner by Lancret.
the elegant figures at their game
of backgammon, in poses of
studied simplicity, evoke the
atmosphere of Marivaux's
comedies.
Right Beaumarchais by Nattier
The painter has not forgotten
that Beaumarchais once taught
music to the ladies of
the royal family.

volving the supply of sixty thousand guns which was to get him into serious trouble. Thrown into prison, released, the object of menaces, he was forced into exile, and he was only able to return to Paris in 1796 where he died three years later at the age of sixty-seven.

The theatre therefore represents only one facet of his tumultuous activity, but his interest in it lasted all through his life and his vitality revelled in it to the full. He was the author of rollicking *parades,* in which he exploited every vein of humour, even the broadest. But he was also tempted to follow in Diderot's foot-steps and try his hand, with varying success, at serious drama on which he published an essay. Nor did he neglect the opera which he planned to transform. However, he owes his fame above all to his two prose comedies – one in four acts and the other in five – *Le Barbier* and *Le Mariage de Figaro.* It is the main character which infuses into both plays, set in a highly fictional, picturesque Spain. Valet to Count Almaviva, then apprentice

apothecary, man of letters, playwright, he has led the picaresque life of an itinerant barber and finally set up in Seville where he runs into his master. Never lacking in high spirits and good sense, he has no illusions, for he knows how things are. There is nobody to touch him for thinking up and carrying out an intrigue. His agility, his wit, his joyous philosophy – 'I hasten to laugh at everything so as not to be forced to cry over it,' (*Barbier,* I, 2) – give the dialogue its rhythm and animation.

The action of *Le Barbier* is relatively simple. It is summed up in the sub-title *ou la Précaution inutile.* 'Brutal, close-fisted, and excessively amorous and jealous' (I, 4), old Bartholo is trying to marry Rosine, his charming young ward. But Count Almaviva is in love with her, and with the help of the ingenious Figaro, after disguising himself as a drunken officer and then as a music master, he finally

In this pen and ink for the *Barbier de Séville* (Act III, scene 4) Bartholo dozes to the sound of the music, while the Count, disguised as Seigneur Alonzo, the pupil and friend of Don Bazile, 'ventures to take the hand of Rosine and covers it with kisses'.

succeeds in marrying her 'in defiance and in the house of her guardian'[69]. *Le Mariage de Figaro* in which the same characters reappear is much more complex. Once he is married, Almaviva proves inconstant, and the very girl whose favours he seeks to obtain is Suzanne, who that very day – the sub-title is *La Folle Journée* – is set to marry Figaro. 'My play', writes Beaumarchais, 'has a diverting interplay of intrigue in which the designing husband, thwarted, worn down, harassed, but still bent on achieving his ends, is obliged, thrice in the course of a single day, to fall at the feet of his wife who . . . ends up by forgiving him'[70]. Figaro has not only the Count to contend with. He is pursued by Marceline who, she swears, has a written promise of marriage from him. It is only at the end of the third act that Marceline and Bartholo turn out to be his parents. What is more, there is Chérubin, the young page in love with all women, with Fanchette, the gardener's daughter, and especially with his godmother, the beauteous countess. He can be relied on to emerge at the drop of a hat from behind a shrub or a sofa throughout the action and wilfully to entangle the strings of the plot. Surprises come thick and fast, and the spectator is borne along in an intoxicating farandolesque movement. The *imbroille,* as the author called it, is at its most furious in the night scenes in the fifth act, in which misunderstandings are legion and make confusion worse confounded until everything is cleared up in the end.

Nevertheless the breathtaking virtuosity of the playwright, who never for a moment allows the audience's attention to flag, is not the whole secret of his success, any more than are the rather transparent characters. What really makes the comedy irresistible is the 'frank old-style [Gallic] gaiety', allied, as the author notes, 'to the light touch of our present humour'[71]. There is a fascinating sense of repartee, the explosive and devastatingly appropriate rejoinders, the priceless sally, the witticisms which bring down the house. In short, a vigorously theatrical verve sweeps the dialogue along. Nobody since Molière had made such striking use of the resources of language and stage by using just the right word or gesture. It is this return to the original, to the fundamental relation between spectator and the characters' words, by which Beaumarchais breathes new life into the theatre.

The most memorable and most profound witticisms have a moral and political punch. These two plays are in fact satires, in the form of a comedy, and there is no mystery about why it took almost as many years and as much effort to obtain permission to perform *Le Mariage de Figaro* as it did for *Tartuffe*. Even at the beginning of *Le Barbier,* Figaro has this dig at Count Almaviva: 'A noble is quite kind enough to us when he does us no harm', and he drives his point home by adding 'Judging by the virtues demanded of a servant, does your Excellency know of many masters fit to be valets?'

(I, 2). A little further on, Bartholo complains of the 'barbarous century' in which he lives. It has, he says, 'produced nothing but idiocies of all kinds – freedom of thought, attraction [of the planets], electricity, tolerance, inoculation, quinquina, the *Encyclopédie* and drama . . . !' (I, 3). Beaumarchais is well aware of the theatre's power to denounce abuses. 'The theatre', he writes, 'is a giant which can mortally wound anything it strikes.' And he goes on to say 'We should keep our heavier blows for public wrongs and evils'[72]. This is exactly what he does in *Le Mariage*. The interest of the famous monologue in the fifth act, one of the longest ever delivered on the French stage, lies almost entirely in the criticism of contemporary French society which Figaro feels very keenly to be absurd and unjust. Almaviva, his unscrupulous rival, is a great nobleman, but what has he done to become one? He has 'taken the trouble to be born, and nothing else . . . Whereas I, damn it', says Figaro, 'lost in the obscurity of the crowd, have had to use more knowledge and calculation simply to get by than was needed in the whole of the last hundred years to govern the wide realm of Spain'. The tirade satirises birth; other passages flay a defective justice, and a subversive ideology gives the verve of the attacks a content which does not however weigh heavily on it. But to be fair, Beaumarchais' stage wine needs no ideological bush. Pure theatre can well make do with the gift, which he possesses in the highest degree, of life and movement.

6 The eighteenth-century novel

Although novels[73] poured off the presses, widely read and sold and sometimes attaining a high level, the genre continued to rank very low in the literary and moral hierarchy of the eighteenth century. An anthologist in the second half of the period who set out to compile what he called the *Library of the Man of Good Taste* prefaced his review of the novels by the admission 'We should like to be able to exclude this whole branch of literature; we know how useless and even how dangerous it is'. And he reminded readers that 'the word "novel" is taken to mean a confused and frivolous assortment of licentious or fanciful adventures calculated less to enlighten the mind than to corrupt the heart'[74]. For his part, Rousseau declares in the preface to *La Nouvelle Héloïse:* 'Never was there a chaste girl who read novels'. And he at once goes on to say that any girl 'who dares to read even a page [of his book] is lost'. As for Voltaire, he was not concerned about the moral aspect of the question. On the literary plane however, despite his *Novels and Tales,* he does not regard the novel as a serious work of art. If he expresses appreciation of the Abbé Prevost, it is only to regret that the author of *Manon Lescaut* should have wasted his talent on such a humble genre. 'I could have wished', he says, 'that he had chosen to write tragedies, for it seems to me that the language of the passions is his natural tongue'[75]. It is obvious that he attaches more importance to the tragedies of the eighteenth century which even when they are by Voltaire himself we no longer rate very highly, than to the extremely attractive novels by his contemporaries.

But the novel did not seem to fare any the worse for this hostility. On the contrary, its absence from the mainstream of literature allowed it to develop a freedom, an originality, a richness of fantasy not to be found in the orthodox genres. As a result it takes on a wide range of forms and displays an astonishing brilliance of invention. While it continues to develop along the lines current in the previous century, there are constant innovations which turn it into the Protean genre as we know it today. Certain writers such as Diderot even indulged in bold experiments which foreshadow the ventures of contemporary writers and 'the new novel'.

What most of the public demanded was above all amusing reading. A common feature of eighteenth-century novels is their high spirits and vividness and the sustained stimulation of interest by an abundance of unexpected events. There was still a marked weakness for the old-style romance. Publishers even re-edited the old novels of chivalry or the ten-volume works of the first sixty years of the previous century. In 1733 *Astrée* appeared in a 'new edition in which the contents and the incidents are left unaltered, and all that has been done is to bring the language up to date and to shorten the dialogues'. But *Astrée* itself is anything but a mere adventure story. It was not only the thirst for adventure which must be satisfied but also the curiosity about people and customs, the interest in psychology and the predilection for ideas – or all these demands at one and the same time.

The wanderings of Le Sage's Gil Blas on the roads of a Spain bearing a curious resemblance to France give him access to most strata of society and to a wide variety of 'characters'. His adventures might just as well be scenes from a comedy of manners, and it is this comedy which forms the most interesting part of the novel. The moralists of the seventeenth century sat in their study whereas Le Sage sends his picaresque hero out into the wide world, but the human subject matter is still the same, and *Gil Blas* can be seen as a La Bruyère tramping along the highways. However, if the portrayal of society and manners is as convincing in this work as in Le Sage's other novels and those of his contemporaries, the characters are flat and lifeless. It was in the psychological novel that the eighteenth century was at its most successful. In this type of work, observations on manners are no less numerous, and the social background is not neglected on that account. The *Illustres Françaises* for example, a series of inter-connected stories which Challes published in 1713, is one of the works in which the concrete life of seventeenth-century Paris is most faithfully and poetically rendered. But the characters have a compelling reality. 'By incontrovertible details', writes Challes in the preface of his novel, 'there is built up in this work a picture of a segment of human relations.' The same holds for the novels of Marivaux and Prévost between 1730 and 1740, of Laclos' novel, *Les liaisons dangereuses* (1782), and indeed of all the great novels of the century. Crébillon in *Le hasard au coin du feu,* or in *La nuit et le moment* (1763) brings off the feat of reproducing as if in slow motion the very movement of feelings, sensations and words (in a scabrous situation), realising what may be regarded as an extreme form of the genre.

Of course the *philosophes* and the ideologists took advantage of the vogue of the novel and of its extreme flexibility and made the most of it as a vehicle for their theories and their propaganda. Montesquieu's *Persian Letters* (1721) are a sort of novel in letter form, but its ideological and polemical significance is immediately obvious. Voltaire wrote his *Philosophical Tales* in the first instance to demonstrate and propagate a certain stock of ideas. Diderot wrote *La Religieuse* and invented, with *Le Neveu de Rameau* and above all with *Jacques le Fataliste,* new media of philosophic investigation and expression. Rousseau clothed his ideology in *La Nouvelle Héloïse* (1762) and, since the subject itself was sentiment, the philosophical validity of his thesis was not unconnected with the literary efficacity of the novel. The same could be said *mutatis mutandis* of Bernardin de Saint Pierre and his exotic and touching novel *Paul et Virginie* (1784), of Restif de la Bretonne and perhaps of De Sade. The whole century is vigorously expressed and accurately reflected in this genre which it succeeded in so modifying as to make of it, as the occasion demanded, a mirror, a work of art or a weapon.

Prévost wrote *Manon Lescaut*
fifteen years before this
engraving of him by Schmidt
was executed. We have no record
of his earlier appearance,
but, as an exile and adventurer,
he cannot have borne much
resemblance to the urbane and
eminently respectable abbé
we see here.

Manon Lescaut

Of all the novels – they run to thirty-nine volumes of his *Selected Works* – composed by the Abbé de Prévost[76] in the course of an eventful life, *L'Histoire du Chevalier Des Grieux et de Manon Lescaut* is still by far the best known. Yet it is only a fragment hived off from a larger novel – *Les Mémoires et Adventures d'un homme de qualité,* of which it forms the seventh and last part published in 1731. True, there was no difficulty about detaching it from the *Mémoires* since the Nobleman hardly figures in it and his role is for all practical purposes confined to acting the attentive and sympathetic listener to Des Grieux's account. But why did later generations fasten on to this piece and forget about all the rest? A possible explanation is that the story is relatively short. Comprising as they do three or four fat volumes, *Le Doyen de Killerine* or *Cleveland,* two of Prévost's other novels which were a great success in the eighteenth

MANON LESCAUT.

Manon gets out of the coach outside
the inn at Amiens. (Illustration by
Dessenne for the 1818 edition.)

147

century, are so long as to put modern readers off. All the same, the
strange and captivating *Histoire d'une Grecque Moderne* and the
tumultuous *Histoire d'un Chevalier de Malte* are hardly any longer
than *Manon*. The real explanation must be sought elsewhere.

The fact is that this short novel, complete in itself, has a capacity
for stirring the heart and a ring of truth which, as we shall see, make
it an out of the ordinary achievement. What touches the reader
right from the start is the natural, direct and engaging manner in
which the Chevalier relates his life story. In this tale, narrated in an
undertone, there is a refusal to indulge in either psychological or
literary effects, a simplicity which sets it poles apart from the
affected or at least stylised nobility of the aristocratic and *galant*
novel, and, at the other end of the spectrum, from the laborious
and prosaic humour of the burlesque and 'realistic' novel. This adventure of the heart which has left its mark for ever on his fate is
recounted unaffectedly by Des Grieux, stage by stage, and the
reader relives it with him in the process. At seventeen and 'never
having thought about the difference of the sexes' (page 19), he meets
Manon who is being packed off to a convent. Her family is 'set in
this way no doubt on putting an end to her search for pleasure which
had already emerged', and which, as the Chevalier observes, 'was
subsequently to be the cause of all her misfortunes and [his]' (page
20). No sooner does he set eyes on her than his passion bursts into
flame. He carries her off and takes her to Paris. But money runs low,
and when he broaches the question of marriage her response is cool.
For she has already made up her mind to surrender to the rich Monsieur de B., the famous farmer-general. It is not long before Des
Grieux is denounced to his father who has him brought back home,
securely guarded. There he spends six months in a sort of seclusion,
weeping for the loss of Manon. But in the end his grief subsides and
he resolves to lead 'a virtuous and Christian life'. If he goes back to
Paris, it is to enter the seminary of Saint Sulpice and stay there.

Manon presents her lover Des Grieux
as her brother to M. de G. M.
Illustration by Gravelot for the 1753
edition of *Manon Lescaut*.

His resolve is in vain. Manon herself comes and seeks him out, and a talk in the seminary parlour is all that is needed to make him forsake everything.

To start with, the two lovers live off the sixty thousand pounds that Manon has extracted from Monsieur de B. over a period of two years. When they are robbed of this money, they subsist on the earnings of Des Grieux who has turned card-sharper. But alas, they are the victims of a second theft, and Manon leaves without telling her lover and offers herself to M. de G.M., 'an old voluptuary who paid lavishly for his pleasures' (page 68). However, Des Grieux manages to persuade her to give up G. M., but she forces him to agree to carrying off the money and jewellery that G.M. was disposed to give her in exchange for her favours. G.M. is furious and has them tracked down. They are soon arrested. The Chevalier succeeds in breaking out of the Saint Lazare prison and killing one of his guards in the process, and he arranges for Manon to escape from hers too. Both of them are happy again, and even, thanks to a number of favourable circumstances, they enjoy a measure of security.

Unfortunately, G.M.'s son, a charming young man, who does not approve of his father's ways, makes their acquaintance and falls in love with Manon. Hand in glove with Des Grieux, she sets out to dupe her new admirer and pretends to accept his generous offers. Indeed she is accepting them in good earnest when the Chevalier catches up with her and persuades her to flee with him – which she does, with the money and the jewellery. Old G.M. is not long in getting to the bottom of the whole business and has them arrested a second time. Des Grieux is soon set free, but Manon is deported with other women of evil repute to the French colonies in America. Her lover gives up everything to follow her to this desert country where misfortune is to dog their footsteps. As it turns out, the governor of New Orleans, who holds undisputed sway over the colony, decides to wrest Manon from Des Grieux in order to give

her to his nephew. The two young people have to take to flight and Manon dies of exhaustion in the desert. Des Grieux falls seriously ill, but in the end he recovers and goes back to France in a desperate mood. It is at this point that he relates his tale to the Nobleman.

Kidnappings, thefts, murders, imprisonments, escapes! At first sight it all looks like an adventure story. In fact we should not be misled by the stormy succession of romantic incidents and sudden twists in the plot. The basic situation is extremely simple and it is always the same. Manon and Des Grieux love each other. But every time that money runs short she accepts the offers of a rich lover who will put her in funds. Thus she thrice deceives or is about to deceive the Chevalier, who for his part cannot stop loving her. As betrayal follows betrayal the consequences become more and more serious, until the final catastrophe is provoked. The two young people thus bring about their misfortunes by means of a psychological mechanism, and it is the study of this process which lies at the heart of the novel. Right at the outset Prévost declares that he proposes to show in Des Grieux 'a terrible example of the power of the passions' (page 4), and on the other hand he invites his readers to reflect 'on the incomprehensible nature of women' (page 15). Manon loves Des Grieux, but she also loves dresses, jewels, amusements. 'Never was a girl less attached than she to money, but she did not have a moment's peace if she was afraid that she would not have enough of it.' (page 61). Now it is so easy for her to procure it by selling her favours! It does not cross her mind that in this way she is failing to observe what she calls the fidelity of the heart, and her complaisances weigh lightly on her. For her love is an affectionate and tender inclination to which one can abandon oneself only if other conditions are fulfilled. For Des Grieux, on the contrary, it is an exclusive passion to which his whole being is committed and everything must be sacrificed. Clearly these two lovers, riveted as they are to each other, do not speak the same language and do not belong to the same species. They go all the more surely to their doom. 'Manon', notes the Chevalier, 'was passionately addicted to pleasure; and I to her.' (page 50).

What Prévost has produced, then, is a tragedy in very truth. No doubt the concentration is not so great as in *Andromaque* or even *La Princesse de Clèves*. The atmosphere is not as stifling and there is not the same feeling of claustrophobia. The exciting developments of the plot keep the air from becoming stale. There are moments when tension flags, and there are even bursts of comedy. But the tragic pattern is still there. The action may be speeded up and incidents piled on incidents, yet the reader's attention is not thereby diverted from the psychological problem that lies at the centre of the novel. Even the setting is as it were abstract, although it could easily have made great play with the picturesque aspects of Regency Paris with its luxury and poverty, its financiers and its dubious characters. Objects have a purely utilitarian function. They are made use of, but are not seen. In *La Grecque Moderne* Prévost, when introducing his reader to a supremely out of the way locality (the Seraglio), merely notes drily 'We went into a place which I need not describe for the purposes of this story'[77]. Nor has he made any greater concession to the false glamour or the demands of the imagination in *Manon Lescaut*. All the limelight is focused on the tragic mechanism which will in the end pulverise the two heroes.

A strange tragic couple, this semi-prostitute and this crook who is a murderer and something of a pimp! How is it that Manon's charm fascinates the reader, that Des Grieux's passionate fidelity touches him, that the sad story of the two lovers moves and obsesses him by its exemplary purity and its freshness? The contemporaries were themselves struck by this paradox. 'It takes consummate art', wrote one of them, 'to arouse our interest in the misfortunes of two such figures'[78]. It does indeed call for a singularly skilful craftsmanship if the two heroes' innocence is not to emerge tarnished from the desperately immoral situations in which they are so often involved. Prévost is at pains to win the reader's sympathy for them. And before long we have Des Grieux's eyes for Manon, who we can imagine as we please and grace with all possible seductions since there is no description of her. She is only presented as 'the sweetest and most loveable creature that ever was' (page 171). As for Des Grieux, he has everything needed to inspire love and esteem – birth, honour, dignity, breeding, basic goodness, prepossessing and noble features, without counting the moving depths of his feelings. There is thus an astonishing contrast. On the one hand, lies, theft, murder, trickery, swindling, prostitution. On the other, an exquisite girl, pretty, tender, all grace and restraint, and with her a young man of good birth, kind, open, generous and faithful. How do these two apparently incompatible worlds of innocence and corruption manage to co-exist in one and the same novel?

One possible explanation is that the unfortunate heroes are the victims of a rotten society which forces them to take part in its infamous activities. Prévost, it is true, dwells on the immorality of the age, on the anti-natural character of a civilisation founded on shameful appetites and unrealistic notions. It is none the less evident that the two young people find no difficulty in adapting themselves very successfully to the depraved milieu in which they live, and that the existence of these circles could at most provide them with attenuating circumstances. The couple's real justification is to be sought in a confused but significant philosophy and in a kind of morality of irresponsibility with which the whole novel is impregnated. In particular Prévost borrows from the Jesuits' casuistry a morality of intention. According to this doctrine, the act in itself does not enable us to pass a moral judgment on the person who commits it, for it is only its intention which gives it a moral significance. Thus Des Grieux does ill, but he remains an honourable man. He never intends to do evil, and every time he does something wrong, he is driven to it by necessity, as can be seen from the murder of his guard whose resistance he has to overcome in order to escape. True, the two lovers are guilty of 'imprudence' and of 'lightheartedness' (pages 148 and 160) but they are excellent creatures at heart. They must not be judged on what they do but on what they *are* – and above all on the richness, on the exceptional delicacy of their sensibility and on their capacity for love. It is sentiment which is at the basis of human values. The innocence of the two heroes lies in their fundamental sincerity and in their bursts of spontaneity.

Unfortunately the flowers of sentiment are poisonous for Des Grieux, and he cannot help plucking and smelling them. Faced with Manon's betrayals, faced with the compromises which she forces on him by her attitude, he falls a prey to grief, vexation, jealousy, and shame, but he is incapable of overcoming his passion. His willpower, he knows not why but has seen it only too clearly from experience, is powerless. 'Can no one explain to me', he asks, 'by what fatal star one is suddenly swept off the course of duty, without being able to put up the slightest resistance and without feeling the slightest remorse?' (pages 42–3). Human freedom is an illusion, and certain passions are irresistible. Is this Greek fate or Christian predestination? He does not know. Every doctrine, every belief will serve his purpose if it can explain his powerlessness and his weakness, and prove his absence of responsibility and thus help to justify him. One must not therefore take too literally the allusions ventured by him to this or that theological doctrine. If he is bent on presenting himself as a tragic hero delivered up to 'the blind fury of a fatal love' (page 61), this is because tragic love seems to him to carry with it a general remission of the sins to which it leads, and to confer a basic dignity which despicable acts cannot destroy. But in fact Des Grieux retains this very dignity. He has no need to play the tragic role as he sometimes does, since his story, as we have seen, is really tragic. It is unfolded in its entirety on the shifting margins of human

The entrance to the *Jardin des Tuileries* seen from Pont Royal. The Tuileries are a favourite walk for Parisians and often figured in the novels of the eighteenth century. (Engraving by J. F. and M. J. Ozanne.)

freedom. *Manon Lescaut* is one of the most complex successes in the French novel. Rarely has the obscurity and the mystery of man been so effectively and so movingly expressed as in the translucent words of this limpid story.

Marivaux's novels

In addition to his early works, Marivaux is the author of two widely differing novels – *La Vie de Marianne* and *Le Paysan Parvenu,* which are set in completely different keys[79]. However, they have this much in common that they are both unfinished and were written in instalments published separately over a period of eleven years in the case of *Marianne* (1731–42) and two in the case of the *Peasant* (1734–5). The novelist, it is clear, did not plan to write a sharply focused story conceived as a whole. He wrote it as a serial, adding

new material all the time, and he did not bother to follow his characters in their evolution until their adventures were over, or in any
case until the reader's curiosity about them was satisfied. True, they
themselves recount their life. They are therefore unable to carry
the account to its natural conclusion and relate their own death.
But they could at least relive the significant events which give their
existence the stamp of destiny and only stop when their life is once
and for all set in an unchanging perspective – in the same way as
Des Grieux's voice is silent once he has retraced the course of his
adventures with Manon and his existence ceases to interest us. Now
this is not at all the case with Marianne. It is only through the sub-
title *(ou les Aventures de Madame la Comtesse de . . .)* that we learn
of Marianne's joining the ranks of the nobility. What has happened
to effect so radical a transformation, the reader will never know. As
for Jacob, the hero of the *Peasant,* we witness the start of his social

ascent, but when the story is abruptly broken off he is very far from having reached his goal. Marivaux's technique, therefore, gives rise to a novel which in a way remains unfinished, an open-ended novel in which the hero makes his way through life unfettered and at his own pace.

Nevertheless, his course is definitely set in a particular direction, and we are all the better able to measure his progress since his starting-point has been more humble and his beginnings more difficult. Marianne does not know who her family was; Jacob cannot count on his. Both are very young and inexperienced when they have to start to fend for themselves on the streets of Paris. How will they extricate themselves from this situation at the start of their career, a situation which has all the appearances of being catastrophic? First and foremost by growing up. Of course, unforeseen events will influence their lives. A whole Parisian picaresque world flows through the novel, incidentally and almost unobtrusively. But these chance incidents are not of themselves very interesting. Their main role is to give the characters an opportunity of feeling, understanding and reacting, in short of transforming themselves. For on coming into contact with people and things, their intelligence and feelings are awakened, their personality is revealed and their character is formed. Both these novels are really *Bildungsromane*, or novels of the years of apprenticeship. Characters take shape and find their feet where earlier they had remained in the limbo of youth, indeed almost of childhood. The atmosphere has the freshness, sometimes even the joyousness of things created new. The driving force of the novel is discovery – the discovery of oneself through the discovery of others and vice versa. In these characters, the knowledge of self and of one's surroundings moves forward simultaneously and in interaction to form an 'experience'. Psychological observation and social portrayal are thus organically linked in the art of the novelist who is more concerned with applying a technique of investigations into human behaviour than with creating a carefully constructed work.

The heart of Marivaux is to be sought in individual or social psychology and not in a plot which has no other purpose than to provide a convenient framework. This is clearly visible in *Marianne*. The heroine's parents, whose identity is unknown, were murdered by highway robbers. The little girl is brought up by a country priest and his sister who have given her a home. At the age of fifteen she finds herself alone and without means in Paris. A wealthy man regarded as pious and charitable, M. de Climal, puts her out with a milliner, Madame Dutour. The following Sunday, Marianne goes to church. There she at once singles out a young man. When mass is over, leaving the church in a reverie she slips in avoiding a coach and hurts her foot. As it happens, the carriage belongs to no other than the young man who has caught her eye, Valville, and he, by an even more surprising coincidence, turns out to be M. de Climal's nephew. The uncle, a dissembling bigot and cynical pleasure-seeker, and the nephew, who has fallen in love with the girl, are thus rivals. Marianne breaks with M. de Climal and leaves Madame Dutour. She seeks refuge in a convent where she is given shelter thanks to the intervention of the lady who happened to be there when Marianne turned up in tears, and who at once took a liking to her. This compassionate lady, we learn to our astonishment, is Valville's mother. Some time later we find Marianne, whose past is kept dark, being treated as a young lady of high birth who is to marry Valville. All of a sudden, Madame Dutour turns up in a house to which Marianne has been invited, offering fabrics and dresses for sale. Obviously, the supernatural and slightly puerile nature of these far-fetched coincidences does not in the least worry the reader. On the contrary, the unexpected element in the story amuses him. They are there to create situations which enable Marianne's personality to be brought out and displayed, and herein lies the real interest of the novel.

Of unknown but – she is convinced – high birth, Marianne is

young, beautiful, intelligent; she has refinement, 'sentiment', dignity and pride. As her benefactress puts it, she is 'noble, generous and disinterested' (page 324). In short she is adorned with all the virtues usually attributed to a character in a novel. Besides, this is how she portrays herself and her life 'in a style that was as noble as it was tragic' to a girl whom she met at the convent: 'I spoke', she comments, 'as a pitiable victim of fate, as a heroine of a novel, who yet spoke nothing but the truth, but who embellished the truth with everything that might make it appear touching and arouse consideration for my misfortune' (page 356). *Who yet spoke nothing but the truth.* In fact, the events in her life have the ring of the most conventional romanticism. This being so, how is it that Marivaux manages to make Marianne come alive so startlingly? By conferring on her a three-dimensionality and a depth which are brought out by her contradictions and her problems, and by endowing her with a lucidity and penetration which enabled him to explore her psychology at leisure. The girl's frankness and generosity of character are not without deviousness nor indeed calculatedness. To start with, she tries to blind herself to M. de Climal's guilty intentions in order to be in a position to go on pocketing his presents. When after her slight accident she is forced to let Valville see her pretty foot, she is happy 'at deriving the immodest profit from the gesture, while retaining all the merit of modesty' (page 67). She tries to put Valville off when he courts her, but she realises that her disinterestedness does not go very far. At times, without actually seeking to take systematic advantage of her virtues, she is close to understanding that maybe after all good deeds are more rewarding than bad ones. Thus, Marianne is neither a story-book princess nor a schemer. She has a keen mind and is not taken in. She sees through herself and other people. Her nobility, which is of the heart, is genuine and reserved. Marivaux, having originally drawn his character from the artificial world of the traditional novel, manages by slight and subtle touches and by consciously avoiding stylisation to create a perfectly balanced and convincing character, and to infuse life into a creature whose reactions are always just right, and exquisitely so.

The case of Jacob is perhaps at the other extreme, but corresponds to Marianne's. The same technique of standing back to assess himself is to be found here too, with the same instinctive intelligence, the same 'sentiment', the same perspicacious self-analysis that is both candid and wily. This jovial, gluttonous, good-natured fellow, who has come up to Paris from the depth of the country to take service in his squire's town house, is a variation of the traditional valet. It is really a reversal of the established order for a character such as he, who has certainly nothing aristocratic or romantic about him, to become the hero of a novel. The work is in fact an anti-novel which goes back to Scarron or Furetière, a novel turned inside out, a burlesque. Now we all know that, in this kind of parodistic and satirical novel, the dull, flat necessities of life are brought into play only to explode the elegant world of the conventional novel and to pour ridicule on its affected nobility. This is not the case in Marivaux. Jacob is, it is true, a gay spark, but the merry world in which he lives is not at all one of burlesque buffoonery, with the distortion of reality usually to be found in that type of work. In this case, both persons and objects are recreated in their full flesh and blood reality. Marivaux takes the burlesque convention as his starting point in the case of Jacob, just as in Marianne's case he had taken the romantic convention. With both, given his rejection of ready-made perspectives and artificial colours, he ends up by creating a world of real people and naturalness.

It is an exemplary world in which the situations and the people constitute as it were the living archetypes of a psychology which, despite its staggering diversification, always aims at the universal. The novelist is in fact an observer of human behaviour for whom the picaresque becomes a method of research. He follows his characters through the daily flux of their adventures, and at every point, in a sort of slow-motion analysis, he draws from their predicament the last drop of wisdom. Thus, instead of launching out into maxims or reflections which might well prove to be abstract, hollow or arbitrary, he is able to produce a snapshot of his characters' psychology in what Sartre calls a 'situation'. Marivaux himself at the beginning of his Journal, *Le Spectateur*, makes a distinction between what he calls 'reflecting as a writer', that is 'with no object in mind', deliberately setting himself to this task and (as he terms it) 'thinking as a man', that is, studying the real motivations to be met with in life and available to the novelist. 'Could not the mind of man, when prompted by a chance object or encounter', he asks, 'produce ideas which are more tangible and less far-fetched for us than does this strained exercise in which it indulges when writing?' The plot of a novel, if we may draw on a metaphor which Stendhal was later to use, is designed to beat back the game towards the psychological hunter. It succeeds in doing so easily and naturally, for Marivaux confesses to us 'I was born with a disposition which makes everything matter for reflection; it is, as it were, an inborn philosophy which I have worked out and which the slightest object sets in motion'. What is admirable is that with such a vocation he never sacrifices the sense of the novel (which is infallible and constant) to the geometrical concept. Both his novels constitute an original and probably unique combination of existentialist feeling and the reflecting mind.

Les liaisons dangereuses

The 'detestable work', the 'impure novel' of this 'monster of immorality', as one of Laclos'[80] contemporaries termed his book, conjures up in most minds a picture of the corrupt French society of the later part of the eighteenth century. It is true that this novel on seduction was published in 1782, and has often been held up as conclusive proof of the licentiousness which, it is asserted, ushered in the collapse of the old régime – in other words, the French Revolution. The book, to quote one of the survivors of this period, is 'one of those meteors in a flaming sky heralding disaster at the end of the eighteenth century'[81]. In this historical context, whether real or imaginary, Laclos has inherited a sulphurous and scandalous reputation which has forced his novel underground, banished it from respectable society for part of the nineteenth century and ensured its success in our own time.

Not that a society can really be regarded as innocent when it permits the existence of such people as the Viscount de Valmont and the Marchioness de Merteuil, the two main characters in the book. However, it would be utterly wrong to confuse this couple with the society in which they stage their exploits. If this distinction is not made, the plot of the novel becomes completely meaningless. For what would be the point of the methodical seducer Valmont's campaign of corruption in an already corrupt world? And where is the daring in defying the taboos of society if they have been already done away with, if anything goes (or almost anything) and the risk is nil? All this emerges clearly from the film (produced in 1960) in which the novel was brought up to date, and transposed into our own permissive age. The story becomes as trite as it is anodyne and boils down to a chronicle of seasonal sleeping around in a big winter sports hotel. Laclos, on the contrary, puts the whole emphasis on the dangers which ceaselessly beset his characters, whether victims or villains, as a result of the vigilance of a society which was infinitely more severe and intransigent than our own. If the modern reader is to grasp the real significance of the novel, he must place it in its contemporary setting with its relatively severe social morals.

The campaigns of seduction which form the essence of the action are part of a sport which calls for a bold approach to psychology,

La petite loge. A dancer is presented by her 'mother'
to a young nobleman. This is a typical scene from
'the life of the fashionable man about town, otherwise
known as a petit-maître'; it is contemporary with
Les Liaisons Dangereuses. (Engraving by Patas
after Moreau le Jeune, 1783.)

great tactical skill and consummate hypocrisy. Every woman realises
that, if she succumbs and her downfall is made public, she will be
immediately dishonoured. Seduction for her means social death and
ostracism. She will have to retire to a convent or languish on her
country estates. And indeed she will be lucky if her family does not
have her locked up. The sport is not only difficult but dangerous. De
Prévan, an unlucky seducer, caught red-handed as a result of the
machinations of the Marchioness de Merteuil, is obliged to leave
the army, though a brilliant officer, and everybody slams the door
in his face. A similar fate awaits Valmont, who like his fellow sedu-
cers must always stand ready to fight a duel with an avenger of
virtue or a rival. And in fact this is how he will meet his end. He is
perfectly well aware that, if his intrigues are denounced, he will
immediately be driven into exile. And even then he will still run the
risk of the French court seeking to extradite him from the foreign
court where he has taken refuge (Letter CLII).

In the double seduction set out in the novel, therefore, the
characters involved stake their happiness, their life and their fate.
And all four of them will lose their reason for living or their life
itself. What starts as a pastime for clever rakes is soon transformed
into a tragedy. The Marchioness de Merteuil is a young widow who,
while cynically indulging in exacting pleasures, succeeds in passing
as a virtuous woman. Wishing to be avenged on the Count de
Gercourt, a lover who abandoned her, she asks her friend, accomplice and former lover the Viscount de Valmont to seduce (before her
marriage) the girl to whom Gercourt is engaged, Cécile de Volanges,
a stupid but attractive blonde straight out of the convent.

At the time Valmont is absorbed in an extremely arduous venture, so arduous indeed as to appear impossible: the seduction of
the virtuous and devout wife of a magistrate, Madame de Tourvel.
But Cécile and Madame de Tourvel are, as it happens, both staying
at the country castle of an old aunt of Valmont's, and he decides to

pursue both intrigues at the same time. He will succeed in his plans. And the reader is enabled to follow, step by step, his intricate manoeuvres. The novel is in letter form. Valmont sends the Marchioness a kind of diary of his progress. His victims' letters are also reproduced, thus showing the events in a different perspective.

To get the better of the simple-minded Cécile, Valmont need only have resort to the usual bag of tricks and a great deal of audacity, especially as he makes himself out to be the Chevalier Danceny's friend, who has been able to win her heart. But when it comes to Madame de Tourvel he has to deploy a much more subtle psychology and more sustained efforts for he clearly cannot succeed unless by gaining her love. As soon as he has seduced her, he abandons her with the utmost boorishness, as the rules of the sport demand. For, as we have seen, the aim is to *ruin* women. Madame de Tourvel dies of a broken heart. Danceny, for his part, when he learns that he has been made a mock of by Valmont, challenges him to a duel and kills him. Cécile withdraws to a convent. Madame de Merteuil is unmasked and flees to Holland.

It is certainly a strange game, this systematic seduction. There is something about it of the chase and the *Kriegsspiel,* or 'war game'. Valmont issues 'despatches' – he uses this very word (XXV) – on his operations. He compares himself to Turenne and Frederick the Great. After the event, he proceeds to make a critical appraisal of his achievements, and comes to an extremely favourable conclusion as regards his strategy in Madame de Tourvel's seduction: 'I have forced the enemy to stand and fight when she only wanted to dally. I have wrested from her the choice of terrain and of tactics' (CXXV). The important point, however, is not the victory. The seducer could hardly care less about 'the insipid advantage of having had one more woman' (XXIII). Valmont is primarily interested in the psychological technique employed, and he means to succeed without cheating: 'Let the obscure poacher, from the safety of his hiding

Madame de Tourvel kneels to Valmont. He describes the scene
to Madame de Merteuil in Letter XCIX: 'But she, taking my hands,
which she covered with tears, sometimes even clasping my knees . . .'
That this picture was not intended for any edition of *Les Liaisons
Dangereuses* shows that the novel had become almost a household name.
(Engraving by Girard after Lavreince, 1785.)

place, kill the stag which he has taken by surprise; a real hunter must bring the stag to *bay*.' (XXIII). The essence of seduction lies in the form; it is not a question of solving the problem at any cost, no matter by what stratagems. The solution must be according to the rules admitted for the purpose of demonstration and be as elegant as possible. Valmont underlines his 'purity of method' (CXXV). His, it will be seen, is a strictly intellectual type of action, and it is aesthetic to the extent that it achieves the perfect adaptation of the intellectual process to the aim pursued so that the work might aptly be called *On seduction considered as one of the fine arts*. For Valmont, libertinage does not consist in taking the easiest course and revelling in facile pleasures. What he seeks is the *attainment* of his pleasure rather than pleasure as such. In short, it is the satisfaction of an exacting and rigorously planned will and not a mere caprice. Seduction is thus portrayed as a pure exercise of the will.

On the ruins of the generally accepted moral values of sincerity and the respect of one's neighbours, the seducer hoists the banner of other values – lucidity and will-power. The characters in the novel are just as monstrous psychologically as they are morally. These heroes of self-mastery who, like Valéry's Monsieur Teste, have 'killed the puppet in them', i.e. have suppressed their automatic reflexes, are all the time conscious of their acts and coolly give them the desired direction. 'Never since his earliest youth', we learn of Valmont, 'did he take a step or say a word without having an end in views . . . His conduct flows from his principles'. Of course, the passage goes on to explain that 'he never had a plan which was not dishonest or criminal' (IX). The tension and masterly skill in Madame de Merteuil's conduct are even more extraordinary. She has succeeded, she confides to her accomplice, in regulating 'the various movements of [her] face . . . I have carried zeal', she adds, 'to the point of deliberately causing myself pain in order to seek to express pleasure at the same time. It is thus that I have managed to gain the control over my expressions at which I have so often seen you astonished' (LXXXI). Valmont and Madame de Merteuil exercise constant control over themselves and ceaselessly repress the promptings of spontaneity and naturalness. They practise what is in effect a kind of asceticism – a satanical asceticism.

The inhuman greatness of such an undertaking might exercise a dangerous fascination on the reader if the characters were capable of sustaining their part. But it is soon clear that, despite the theories which he so complacently sets forth, Valmont is in fact in love with Madame de Tourvel. The intellectual experiment of seducing her is thus falsified at the root. He is even within an inch of jettisoning his calculating plans under the spell of this delightful woman who has 'given him back', he tells us, 'the enchanting illusions of youth' (VI). It is Madame de Merteuil who makes fun of him and recalls him to the paths of his absurd duty. Valmont, worn out and jaded, sacrifices on the altar of his impossible role his only chance of salvation – this unhoped-for love which might perhaps have made his 'blighted heart' blossom again. Madame de Merteuil realises this. She is jealous of her rival and is out to punish Valmont. 'Yes, Viscount', she writes to him, 'you were very fond of Madame de Tourvel, and indeed you are still in love with her, madly in love; but, because I amused myself shaming you out of it, you sacrificed her without a moment's hesitation.' (CLXV) Valmont's tragedy is not that he dies, but that, deliberately, and irrevocably, he destroys himself to satisfy his intellectual vanity and pride.

It follows that the superiority of the two main characters is no more than a mirage. They aspire to rise above ordinary humanity, but they are in fact usually guided by the common-or-garden sentiments of love and jealousy. By portraying the tragedy of the twilight world between eroticism and will-power in a marvellously descriptive and appropriate language, Laclos has fashioned one of the most intelligent novels of world literature.

7 Literature and the Enlightenment

'Anyone born a Christian and a Frenchman', La Bruyère had noted at the end of the seventeenth century, 'is subject to certain constraints when it comes to satire. He is debarred from the major themes'[82]. And in fact the Catholic church and the absolute monarchy did not encourage writers to be outspoken, especially when it came to questioning religious dogmas or the political régime. Boileau's satires hardly did more than launch a few innocuous shafts at various vices or foibles and repeat a number of moral commonplaces which he shared with the preachers of the age.

While the century which produced Descartes and the *libertins* (i.e. freethinkers) was certainly not lacking in intellectual daring, it was generally chary of a clear, direct and public approach to the problems which Revelation and the State claimed to have solved once and for all. In those days, literature usually did not aim to do more than please, and that only by literary effects – by the beauty of the language, the charm of the fiction and the subtlety of the analysis, and of course, by making the most of the resources of each of the genres cultivated. Even though implicitly or explicitly Racine's tragedies reflect a metaphysical view of man, or Molière's comedies a conception of man as a social being, or La Bruyère's *Caractères* a criticism of manners, writers in the seventeenth century did not directly question Christian dogma or political institutions.

The situation in the eighteenth century was entirely different. The traditional genres – the novel, the theatre and so on, continued to flourish, but literature tended to become ideological and polemical. It never seems to have occurred to Corneille or La Fontaine that it was their duty to make a methodical study of the society in which they lived and to seek to transform it. Montesquieu, Voltaire and Diderot on the contrary were convinced that every thinking man or woman ought to subject the world he lived in to a critical examination, and, if he could wield a pen, to denounce what appeared to him to be intolerable abuses. From then on conformism, whether

A group of *philosophes* in discussion in
a coffee house. It was the coffee houses –
as salons open to all comers – which
encouraged the spread of new ideas.
(Illustration for *Mémoires Philosophiques
du Baron de* ∗∗∗ by Crillon, 1777.)

Etablissement de la nouvelle Philosophie.
Notre Berceau fut un Caffé.

This *lettre de cachet*, signed by Louis XV, does not show the prisoner's crime or the length of his imprisonment: obviously there was no intention of bringing him to trial. All the *philosophes* protested against this royal despotism which *habeas corpus* made impossible in England.

due to indifference, laziness, prudence or contempt, was severely condemned. Literature was no longer afraid to tackle the 'major themes – religion, philosophy, politics, morals. 'Force me to keep silent on religion and government', exclaims one of Diderot's mouth-pieces, 'and there would be nothing left for me to say'[83].

It was in this intellectual climate that the man of letters adopted the title of *philosophe,* which did not necessarily mean, as is the case nowadays, that he was a student of metaphysical problems, but rather that he concentrated on clarifying the various aspects of scientific knowledge, that he had a social and political creed and conducted an agitation designed, directly or indirectly, to achieve the reforms needed to make society more reasonable and more humane. This was two hundred years before the term 'committed' literature was invented. In a world darkened by ignorance, super-stition and error, this literature did in fact become the vehicle of the Enlightenment, that is, of critical reason based in its turn on know-ledge. And by diffusing what the French called *les lumières* (i.e. light), it did in fact clear the way for a more enlightened world.

The same critical debunking spirit was visible in Fontenelle's *Histoire des Oracles* (1687), which gives a palpable 'demonstra-tion' of priestly imposture, and in Bayle's great *Historical and Critical Dictionary* (1697), an astonishing collection of the idiocies of the traditional mind. Admittedly, the main target of the critical spirit was religious dogmatism and intolerant fanaticism. All the *philosophes* attacked revealed religions, especially Catholicism (or at least the church). But the extent and slant of their criticism, in this field and in that of social and political organisation, showed a great degree of diversity. They were at one almost only in denoun-cing abuses, that is, evil behaviour, practices and institutions which were unjustly foisted on a wretched humanity. And even then the reformers did not always denounce the same wrong. The main abuses, using the word in its broad sense – for they were of very

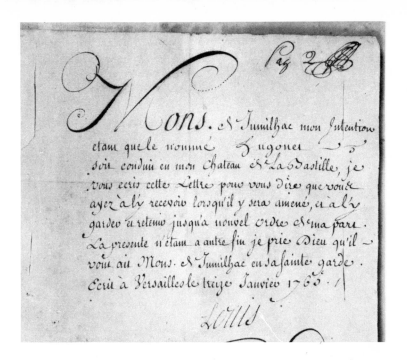

different orders, and it is not possible to draw up a methodical list – were war, slavery, the burnings at the stake by the Inquisition (especially in Spain and Portugal), and (particularly in France) religious intolerance, and the persecution of the Protestants, the muddle and the injustice of the law, the *lettre de cachet* which made it possible to imprison the accused without trial, torture applied to the guilty and even to suspects, censorship and the serious restrictions imposed by it on publishing and so on. In short, the battle of the *philosophes* was waged under the banner of reason, justice, humanity and liberty. It was conducted, writes Diderot, 'by love of virtue, by philanthropy and by the passion for truth, goodness and beauty – a trinity which is a trifle better than the Christian one'. 'Our battle cry', he adds, 'is: No quarter to the superstitious, the fanatical, the ignorant, the mad, the evil and the tyrannical'[84].

But as a rule the *philosophes* acted in scattered bands without co-ordinating their efforts. Voltaire was to deplore this fact in 1763.

Car. Eisen del.   Car.g.auth.er a: acadom. art.Lond. incid. 177.

A plea for racial tolerance: in the foreground Nature, whose six breasts   173
symbolise abundance, nourishes the black child and the white together.
In the background slave dealers drive the population of an African
village into slavery. (Illustration after Eisen for book x of *Histoire
philosophique et politique des établissements et du commerce des
Européens dans les Indes* by Raynal, 1770.)

They ought, he felt, 'to form a compact and impressive organisation instead of acting in isolation when they could easily be cut to pieces by the fanatics and idiots'. The creed of the Enlightenment could act as a rallying point for men of good will. As it was, 'only superstition had the privilege in [his] society'[85]. The only important venture in which the *philosophes,* in one way or another, took part as a body – incidentally with the most admirable disinterestedness – was the *Encyclopédie.* Montesquieu (in the article on Taste), Voltaire, Rousseau (articles on music), the learned D'Alembert, and fifty other remarkable thinkers and specialists were at one point collaborating in the *Dictionnaire raisonné des Sciences, des Arts et des Métiers,* which was directed by Diderot for twenty-five long years of dramatic and at times heroic battles. The idea was conceived about 1745, and a beginning was made in 1751 with the publication of the first two volumes, prefaced by the famous *Introductory Discourse.* Only in 1772 was the work finished – seventeen volumes of text and eleven of plates. Its aim, writes Diderot, 'is to assemble the knowledge scattered over the surface of the earth; to set out the general pattern thereof to our fellow men and to transmit it to those who will come after us, so that . . . our grandsons, as they become better educated, will at the same time become more virtuous and happier'[86]. Human progress and happiness, it will be seen, are linked to the progress and spread of knowledge, and political action to the fight to improve scientific information. For that matter, the *philosophes'* spirit underlying the venture is visible not only in the positivistic approach but also in a veritable crusade which seized on the slightest pretext to further its cause, even in the apparently most anodyne articles – down to the grammatical examples[87]. This balance sheet of contemporary knowledge is seasoned by devastating religious, political and social exposés. This dictionary is more than its title suggests. It is also a piece of heavy artillery and a propaganda manual. It spells out the ABC of the essential reforms. The powers-

174

that-be were not taken in. The first two volumes were banned shortly after publication, and from then on persecution never let up. In 1759 the situation appeared desperate. Indeed, prodigies of patience, skill and courage alone enabled the work to appear.

The *Encyclopédie,* then, like the writings of each of the *philosophes,* constitutes an opposition literature. In the seventeenth century, the court was the centre of good taste and a specifically literary literature. The greatest writers were accorded pensions by the king. In the eighteenth century, an ideological literature took shape outside the bounds of the court and despite the government's hostility. Almost all the books that counted at the time were printed abroad, or clandestinely in France. Foreign sovereigns – Frederick II or Catherine II, 'enlightened despots', proposed to Diderot that he should come and complete the *Encyclopédie* in Prussia or Russia, and the writer was justified in exclaiming 'It is in France, the land of good manners, science, the arts, good taste and philosophy that we are hounded down, and it is from the depths of the barbaric and icy plains of the north that a welcoming hand is extended to help us'[88]. Louis XV's court confined itself to applauding operas. The real intellectual life went on elsewhere, and the discussions leading up to the ideas inspiring this literature, which was often spoken before it was written down, took place in drawing rooms, clubs or cafés, which buzzed with an intense intellectual activity. Despite repeated prohibitions, in a conspiracy of virtue and a crusade for reason, literature resolutely raised the problem of man's place in the world and opened up vistas of action to achieve its objectives.

Montesquieu

A magistrate conscious of his rank and duties – he was one of the presidents of the Bordeaux *Parlement* – and a landowner keen on developing his estates, Charles de Secondat, Baron de la Brède and

de Montesquieu, was essentially a bookworm and a writer[89]. Not
that he did not have a sharp eye for what was going on in his native
Bordelais, or in Paris, or on the travels that took him to England
and Italy. But his thought and reflection were fed mainly by reading,
and they inevitably ended up in writing. He was an indefatigable
worker and toiled away at endless compilations. A good part of his
life was spent wielding a quill. He sought refuge in intellectual effort.
It was even his reason for living. 'Study', he observed, 'has been my
sovereign remedy for the rebuffs of life. There has never been an
affliction which a quarter of an hour's reading could not cure'[90].
Whether he is to be pitied or envied, an existence of this kind is
bound to leave some trace of itself behind. And he took steps to
make sure that it did. He never threw anything away, be it travel
jottings, notes from books he had read, manuscripts, rough drafts,
observations and musings, or, as he called his two scrapbooks,
Pensées and *Spicilège*. He tucked them all away in his papers at
La Brède Castle, or at least much more than was usually preserved by his contemporaries. He made a point of keeping fragments of unfinished works or of those which he had not been able
to fit into his books – passages from a tragedy composed at college,
even his witty remarks. He gives the impression of having tried to
amass in a sort of spasmodically kept intellectual diary the sum of
all he had read or thought. In short, it cannot be said of him that
'he erases the living word'[91]. It would be truer to say that he erased
the written page, or rather that he regarded it as a valuable asset on
which he was subsequently to lean, the substance of an intellectual
heritage to be preserved and developed – which was the expression
and guarantee of the productivity of the mind.

And yet he was not a mere man of letters. His interests went far
beyond anything that might be expected of a connoisseur of literature. 'I am (I think)', he was to note, 'almost the only man to have
written books and yet to have always been afraid of acquiring the

reputation of a drawing room writer'[92]. If he wrote, it was because he had something to say. His speeches and papers to the Academy of Bordeaux, to which he had been admitted in 1716 at the age of twenty-seven, deal with physics, geology, biology and the natural sciences. Between 1718 and 1721, he was to treat among other things, the echo, the adrenal glands, specific gravity and the transparency of bodies. Obviously for his time he answers fairly closely to the idea of a type – fairly common in the eighteenth century – of the provincial magistrate addicted to science. It was in the science of man that Montesquieu was to achieve fame. In that age, there was no clear line of demarcation between philosophy and science and even less of one between the exact and humane sciences. It was in the latter, in the study of the political and social structures – a decided novelty in his days and one which has now developed into a science – that Montesquieu found his real vocation. Those who today continue the search defined and anticipated with such genius in *L'Esprit des Lois* take their cue from science and not from literature.

However, there is one work in which this ideological quest blends felicitously with the perfect literary vehicle: the *Persian Letters* which he published in 1721. If the philosophical thought appears somewhat lacking in depth, it is because this brilliant book was meant to appeal to a society audience, and hence to be frivolous. The exotic is shamelessly exploited. The reader is initiated by the complacent author into the intrigues of the harems of Persia and the piquant secrets of oriental eroticism. Montesquieu aims at a bland elegance, takes pains with his style and calculates his effects. This ingenious presentation largely explains the book's immense success.

Two Persians, newly arrived in France, look with an unjaded eye at the people, customs and institutions of the country which they are in the process of discovering. These foreigners belong to another world. For them what is customary is not always what is necessary or rational, as is all too often the case for Frenchmen living in

France, who cannot conceive of a moral, social and political system other than the one in which they have grown up. And the Persians play havoc with that system. The veil of the conventions is rent; prejudices are unmasked; stupidity and absurdity are stripped of the venerable veneer of tradition overlaying them. A whole society, possibly a whole civilisation, is called in question and exposed to derision. The astonishment of the Frenchman (in Letter xxx) who asks naïvely 'How can anyone be a Persian?' is matched by the astonishment of the two Persians. Theirs is a revolutionary reaction: how can anyone be a Frenchman? How can anyone accept the world as it is at present? Between the Persian who has chanced to be born in a far-off country and the daily scene in France there is a gap – a gap caused by thought itself. By this device, the reader is afforded the detachment needed to judge these values and to judge himself. This 're-angling' machine, the secret formula for which it was easy to work out, was soon to be exploited by a host of imitators.

The examination of French life as seen through the eyes of the two Persians ranges from light mockery to radical subversion. The digs at human foibles, customs and fashions, and at types of man in social life, do not always go very deep, and we have the impression that the Persians have been reading too much of La Bruyère's *Caractères*. But the humour is more acid than in the moralist's work. More diverting, too, as they are out to poke fun at their butt; and the observation is given a completely new twist thanks to the deftness of the narration, the boldness with which the sketches are dashed off and the vividness of the comic scenes. There is a note on the streets of Paris: 'Since I got here a month ago, I have not yet seen anyone going for a walk in the street. There is no people in the world that gets more out of their frame than the French. They run, they fly' (xxiv). Or there is an epigram: 'The French hardly ever refer to their wives; it is because they are afraid of speaking about them in front of people who know them better than they themselves do'

(LV). And in fact the women are all coquettish, perpetually absorbed in beautifying themselves and trying to look younger. In Letter LV, we are given a glimpse of a gathering of women aged respectively twenty, forty, sixty and eighty. Each of them feels that the toilette of the next oldest is ridiculous, but wishes to be taken for the sister of the next youngest to her. This attitude provides the material for a series of skits which are highly diverting although the mechanics employed are rather obvious. Letter XLVIII contains a gallery of portraits. A few sentences suffice to give a thumbnail sketch of the absurd, odious and inconsistent behaviour of the opulent tax-farmer, the officious spiritual director, the starveling poet, the crusty old warrior, the ladies' man who 'talks louder than all the rest and is so glad he is alive'.

But as often as not the visitors' criticisms overstep the bounds of the permissible and leave the safe territory of generic satire for the dangerous regions of politics and religion. Montesquieu is not content merely to denounce Law's famous system which played havoc with the fortunes of so many, plunging some into destitution and raising others to new heights of scandalous wealth. He does not stop at the observation 'The lackeys' trade union commands more respect in France than elsewhere; it is a nursery of great lords' (XCVIII). He hits out at the royal system of administration, at its financial manipulations, at its repeated devaluations: 'The king here is a great magician! He holds sway over the *minds* of his subjects. He makes them think whatever he wishes. If he has only a million crowns in the treasury, and he needs two million, he has only to persuade them that one crown is worth two and they believe him' (XXIV). He has no hesitation in stressing the curious contradictions between the welfare of the court and that of the State. Often, he notes, the king 'prefers the man who undresses him or who hands him a napkin to another who conquers towns and wins his battles' (XXXVII).

The attacks on the Christian religion are even more daring. The

The newswriters, an anonymous
caricature. A curious audience listens
to a reading of the *Gazette* in a public
garden. Interest in the opinions
of the press increased throughout
the eighteenth century.

head of the church is 'an ancient idol at whose shrine people burn
incense out of habit' (XXIX). In the same letter in which the king is
termed a magician, the pope is portrayed as 'another magician, but
an even stronger one, who is no less master of the king's mind than
he himself is of other people's; at times, he makes them believe that
three are only one, that the bread one eats is not really bread, or
that the wine one drinks is not wine, and scores of other things of the
sort'. And so, the basic Catholic dogmas of the Trinity and transub-
stantiation are dismissed as quaint illusions of the human mind, or
as colourful folklore. The church is not even able to keep the peace
between the faithful; it is perpetually rent by theological disputes.
'There has never been a kingdom more plagued by civil war than
the kingdom of Christ.' (XXIX). With the Inquisition, these battles
take on a particularly savage intensity in Spain and Portugal, for
then they are waged by 'certain dervishes who will stand for no
nonsense and who send men to the stake to be burned like a hay-
rick' (XXIX). The relativity of everything affecting man's estate does
not spare religion. Men have formed their gods in their own image.
'When I see men crawling about on an atom [that is, the earth],
which is but a speck in the universe, who dare to put themselves
forward directly as models for Providence, I cannot conceive how
such petty creatures can be so preposterous.' (LIX).

Must we then succumb to scepticism and simply laugh at the
follies of mankind – if we are not to wax indignant at them? Does
Montesquieu blithely blow a whole world to smithereens with
ridicule and leave his readers sitting disconsolate among the ruins?
Not at all. For him, doubt has a philosophic function. It makes a
clean sweep of everything. But its purpose is not to breed nihilism.
It is to point the way to a new order. Montesquieu puts deism in
Christianity's place – and its main imperative is to 'observe the rules
of society and the duties of humanity' (XLVI). As for political and
social institutions, he is not content to demolish them beneath a

hail of witticisms and shattering observations. He studies these institutions in a constructive spirit, and avoids the naïve error of seeking to reform them on paper. He does not go beyond the formulation of certain central principles – in the Utopian vision of the Troglodytes which is set out in four Letters (XI to XIV). For the rest, he remarks, 'there is sometimes a case for altering the law. But such cases are rare, and, when they do occur, we should only take action with a trembling hand' (CXXIX). Behind the façade of a satirical and occasionally licentious novel, the *Persian Letters* is really a serious work, in which Montesquieu already chalks out the theses which he was later to develop and which foreshadow his major, lifelong goal – the search for, and the study and explanation of, the laws governing all the different types of society.

In the *Persian Letters* his aim in fact is not to judge or even to condemn, as so many bitter gibes might lead one to believe, but basically to understand. The best system, he affirms, 'is the one that pursues its goal at the smallest expense, so that the most perfect government is the one that steers men in the direction most in accordance with their inclinations' (LXXX). It is not possible therefore to judge an institution or a custom in itself. It must be judged by the extent to which it conforms to the spirit of the people concerned. To take a particular case, Montesquieu does not pass judgment on duels, a burning issue at the time. But he brings out the painful conflict between the law which bans them and the pressure of opinion which insists on their retention. The 'code of honour, in fact, obliges a gentleman to seek revenge when he is the victim of a slight, yet justice metes out severe punishment on him when he obtains satisfaction. If you follow the code of honour, you perish on the scaffold; if you follow the precepts of official justice, you are banished for ever from human society. You are left in the cruel dilemma of dying or being deemed unworthy to live.' (XC). With the same objectivity he examines the various manifestations and causes of depopulation, about which he is particularly concerned (CXII to CXXII). Or, to take another example, there is the relation between technical progress, particularly the art of war, and history. 'I tremble perpetually,' he writes, 'lest someone discover a more expeditious way of destroying men, peoples and even whole nations' (CV). But he sees grounds for re-assurance. 'If such a deadly invention were discovered, it would soon be banned by the law of nations, and the unanimous verdict of humanity would order its burial.' (CVI). In another disquisition, he recalls the role of parliaments in a monarchy (XCII), or he gives an outline of 'the history and origin of republics' (CVI). In short, a whole political philosophy and, even more, a method for the application of this approach, can be deduced from the *Persian Letters*. The novel may give the impression of being only intellectual fireworks, but the glow is already that of the Enlightenment.

Montesquieu was not long in realising the originality of his research, and he devoted himself to it wholeheartedly. In the *Considérations sur les causes de la grandeur des Romains et de leur décadance,* which he published in 1734, he tried to single out the necessary and illuminating relations between historical facts and the customs and institutions of the Romans at the time in question. The way was now open for the work which was to dominate his intellectual activity-*L'Esprit des Lois* (1748). The idea at the heart of this gigantic inquiry covering all nations in all ages is that the customs, the political life and even the type of government – despite their different character, oddities and contradictions – are not the work of caprice or chance. They have a meaning. As we read in the preface to the book: 'I first of all studied mankind, and it seemed to me that, in this endless welter of laws and customs, men were not guided solely by their fantasies'. Both Christian and sceptical thinkers had more often than not seen eye to eye in denouncing the frailty and corruption of man. Humanity, they felt, was embarked on the Ship of Fools.

Montesquieu's genius lay in making sense of the apparent arbitrariness and madness of life in society, and hence he forthrightly declared that it was possible to describe that world, to study it and explain it in the same spirit as that applied to the physical sciences. He was thus one of the founders of sociology, of political science and, to go even further, of the science of man.

For Montesquieu the laws are 'the necessary relations flowing from the nature of things' (Book I, chapter 1). Unlike physical laws, political and civil laws are not always observed or can be changed, yet they exist. Their extreme diversity is due to the fact that 'they are bound to be related to the physical nature of the country – to the climate (whether icy, torrid or temperate), to the nature of its soil, to its geographical situation, to its size, and to the people, be they ploughmen, hunters or shepherds. These relations must also be linked up with the degree of liberty which the constitution can tolerate; with the inhabitants' religion, their inclinations, their wealth, their numbers, commerce, morals and manners. Lastly the relations are themselves interconnected. They are affected by their origin, by the lawgivers' aims, by the order of things on which they are based' (chapter 3). All these relations, in their totality, form 'what is called the *spirit of the laws'*, that is to say, a certain logic of interrelations in the social and political field. The work, then, consists in the methodical study of these different relations, the nature and interplay of which define, determine or influence the laws.

A key relation is the one between the law and the form and operation of each type of government. There are three types: the *republican,* which can be democratic (as in ancient Athens and Rome) or aristocratic (in the Venice of the Doges); the *monarchic,* 'in which there is a single ruler but one who is subject to fixed and established laws' and respects 'the intermediary powers' (e.g. the nobility, the clergy and the *parlements* etc.); and the *despotic* type, in which 'a single ruler, unrestrained by laws or principles, sweeps all before him by his wishes and his whims' (II). Thus, the nature of a government is 'what makes it be as it is'. Its indwelling principle, on the contrary, is 'what makes it act as it does'. Its nature lies in its structure, its principle in the human passions which provide its driving power (III, 1). The principle underlying a popular or republican state is *virtue,* that is, 'the love of the laws and the fatherland with a continual preference for the general interest over one's own' (IV, 5). The motive behind monarchic government is *honour,* or the concern that everyone should have for his rank and dignity, his adherence to the social hierarchy, as well as his desire to secure recognition and distinction from his hierarchical superiors. Finally, 'in a despotic government, *fear* is an essential ingredient' (III, 9). Asiatic despotism is utterly uninterested in honour. As the *Persian Letters* had earlier put it, 'despair at dishonour overwhelms a Frenchman condemned to a punishment which would not deprive a Turk of a quarter of an hour's sleep (LXXX).

By these comprehensive equations, Montesquieu creates a political algebra which he need merely apply (it would seem) to any specific laws in order to provide its explanation. He even seems to be carried away by the vertigo of a vision whereby the universe becomes clear and transparent to the conquering intellect, for he proudly proclaims in his preface 'I have laid down the principles and beheld particular cases comply with them, effortlessly, and the history of all nations follow automatically from them . . .'. In fact, this deductive rationalism is more apparent than real, and it can at times be reduced to an expository technique. 'I have not drawn my principles from my prejudices', we read, again in the preface, 'but from the nature of things.' This passage indicates an inductive rather than a deductive approach. The prodigious range of facts and problems has forced the author to adopt a plan which has neither the clarity nor the aesthetic balance of a purely formal rationalism. There are 31 books of which the twenty-eighth contains 45 chapters running to 75 pages in all, whereas the twenty-seventh book contains only a single chapter of 12 pages. It is obvious that Montesquieu did not try to fit his material into a regular, formal pattern, but followed where his subject led him. Instead of a mathematically perfect but possibly hollow analysis, the book is a fascinating labyrinth in which experience is perpetually fed into the general thesis, and facts and theories are superbly blended.

But the main emphasis is on the theories. These seem at times to be self-sufficient and to retain their epistemological value independently of the facts involved. Nor is this entirely accidental. For Montesquieu does not always take the trouble to verify his facts, and there are grounds for supposing that he sometimes adduces them simply in order to trot out his explanation. Thus in the *Considérations* it did not occur to him, as it had done to some of his contemporaries, to question the traditional version of early Roman history. And in *L'Esprit des Lois* he does not seriously attempt to ascertain whether there is really a law establishing polyandry among the warriors of the Malabar coast – which, however, he promptly proceeds to explain: 'In Europe, soldiers are prevented from marrying. In Malabar, where the climate is more stimulating, marriage has merely been made as little of a tie as possible. One wife has been allotted to a number of men' (xvi, 5). He does not seem to realise that the explanation has a greater impact when the facts are accurate and have been checked. But fortunately he is fairly often careful to do so, and he even draws on his own experience for the purpose. Thus he observes, talking of the influence of the climate, 'As climates are distinguished by the degree of latitude, they might also be distinguished, so to speak, by the degree of sensibility'; and notes 'I have seen opera in both England and Italy. The same compositions and the same actors; yet the same music produces such utterly different effects on the two nations as to leave one dumbfounded. The on remains calm; the other goes into ecstasies' (xiv, 2).

If he is not always at pains to make sure of his facts, he at least avoids making value-judgments. He declares 'I am not writing to censure the established practice in any particular country' (Preface). He is neither historian, moralist, nor reformer, but a jurist and a sociologist. 'Every nation', he writes, 'will find in these pages the reasons underlying its laws.' The only judgments which he insists on making are of consistency, that is, he determines whether the laws are adapted to the land or the nation and whether they are satisfactorily applied. He had already noted during his travels: 'When I visit a country, I do not try to ascertain whether the laws are good, but whether the existing laws are carried out, for the laws are good everywhere you go'[93].

But Montesquieu, in tackling so many burning issues, is not always the cold, impassive observer. He is not deaf to the 'voice of nature' (VI, 17). He makes a stand whenever possible in favour of the Enlightenment's principles. He condemns negro slavery, observing with barbed irony: 'It is impossible to suppose that these people are men. For, if we did, we would begin to believe that we ourselves are not Christians' (XV, 5). He denounces the use of torture in criminal interrogations (VI, 17). He flays the Inquisitions in his *Most humble remonstrance to the Inquisitors of Spain and Portugal* (XXV, 13). He emphasises the duty of the State to provide welfare services (XXIII, 29). He shows the dangers and the absurdity of the armaments race (XIII, 17). In short he is not a whit behind the other *philosophes* when it comes to humanitarian generosity of soul.

But his influence is all the greater because he does not come forward in the guise of a partisan and because his aim is manifestly to understand, not to overthrow, the political scheme of things. The first phase of the French Revolution (that of the jurists) was directly inspired by him. He is one of the founders of the modern world. We need only recall his definition of liberty, so novel at the time: 'Political liberty does not consist in doing what one wants. Liberty is the right to do everything the law permits. If a citizen could do what the law forbids, he would not thereby achieve greater liberty, since all the others would have exactly the same permission' (XI, 3). Or there is the remark, even more revolutionary in 1748, about work: 'A man is not poor because he possesses nothing, but because he does not work' (XXIII, 29). Even if some of his views are nowadays contested or outdated, it must be recognised that rarely has a thinker defined with such prescience the principles underlying future régimes, or, even more remarkably, a scientific method which, after a lapse of over two centuries, is proving more fruitful than ever.

Voltaire

His huge work[94] – multiform, varied and sprawling – spans the whole eighteenth century, over which he reigned more supremely than did Louis XV. It extends upwards of over sixty eventful and occasionally dramatic years of a long existence (1694–1778). Voltaire is first and foremost a writer. He thought, felt, created, acted and lived, pen in hand. He is there, warts and all, with his impulses, his limitations, his cast of mind, his obsessions, his big-heartedness and his incomprehensions, in the seventy volumes of the Kehl edition, published by Beaumarchais (1784–9), or in the seventy-two volumes of the Beuchot edition (1830–40) and in the hundred and seven volumes of his recently published *Correspondence* (1953–67). A superbly agile mind, a truly encyclopedic curiosity and a prodigious virtuosity go to make up this vast mass of literature for, even when relaxing in the informality of his familiar letters, Voltaire remains a writer – and often a better one than in his more carefully polished works. He cultivated all or most of the known literary genres, and, what is more, he conferred lustre on new ones. He explored every field of human reflection – science, philosophy, religion, manners, history, politics and economics, often it is true, with seven-leagued

Voltaire aged eighty-three.
(Engraving after Huber, 1777.)

boots, and his enemies denounced him as a populariser, an over-simplifier and a jack of all trades. When he is brief, it is almost always because an effective demonstration requires it, because the man of action has the *philosophe* in tow. And generally speaking he is accurate and well-informed[95].

Even before he was forty, he came to the conclusion that a writer must above all be a fighter in the cause of the Enlightenment, striving to change the face of his times. While acutely responsive to the joys of the theatre, to the charms of light verse, or to the specifically literary pleasures of the well-turned phrase, Voltaire, as a perfect man of letters, never let himself be carried away by words. He never wrote for the sake of writing; he wrote to influence the age in which he lived. Monologues were alien to his character. He always had the public in mind, and his aim was to please, scandalise, persuade or arouse to indignation. Far from seeking to escape from his age, he was more often than not in the thick of contemporary controversy. If he steered clear of Paris for much of his life, it was certainly not in order to take refuge in a philosopher's ivory tower; on the contrary, it was to ensure his safety and to give him greater freedom to intervene in current affairs. From 1717 to 1718 he was imprisoned in the Bastille. From then on he was to take the necessary precautions and, when danger threatened, to take cover behind pseudonyms or anonymity, and put the right distance between authority and himself. After his period of exile in England (1726–8), he spent long stretches during the ten years following 1734 in France, at Cirey, not far from the then frontier, in the castle of his friend the Marquise du Châtelet. In 1750 he set out for the court of Frederick II of Prussia (Frederick the Great) where he remained for almost three years. From that time until 1778 (the year of his death) he never returned to Paris. After 1760, he resided in lordly splendour at Ferney in France, a stone's throw from Geneva, a strategically excellent place for both geographical and political reasons. For almost twenty years, exploiting his tactical liberty to the full, he was to launch an almost daily avalanche of letters, lampoons, and pamphlets, whether ponderous tomes or slender brochures, such as turned this obscure village into one of the intellectual capitals of Europe and a mecca of the Enlightenment.

But, before he became the leading thinker of the age and tutor to mankind, Voltaire was just a writer following cheerfully in the footsteps of the masters of the seventeenth century. The epic, that century-old dream of the French poets, was the height of every author's ambition, and accordingly Voltaire composed *La Ligue* (1723) which he was shortly to re-christen *Le Henriade* (1728). In this work, he recounted the religious and civil wars in which from 1589 to 1594 Henri IV distinguished himself. The poet observes most of the conventions of the genre. He makes lavish use of mythology and allegory, even arranging for a descent to Hades and peppering his pages with rhetorical figures and flourishes. It was a huge success. Yet, despite his epic laurels, Voltaire was essentially a dramatist. He had a lifelong passion for the theatre. In the *Encyclopédie* (the article on Geneva), D'Alembert proposed that a theatre be opened in Calvin's hometown. Voltaire was not unconnected with this suggestion, which many people regarded as unseemly and which led Rousseau to publish his *Lettre sur les Spectacles* (1758). It was *Oedipe,* a tragedy performed in 1718, that first made Voltaire's name. He was then only twenty-four. Sixty years later, the performance of his tragedy *Irène* (30 March 1778) marked his apotheosis. As confirmed addicts of the theatre who were fascinated by Corneille and Racine, his contemporaries acclaimed him as the successor and emulator of those two playwrights, thought to be unsurpassable. But he was far from being a mere epigone. He struck out in new directions. True, he stuck to the five-acter in verse and to the classical seventeenth-century rules, but, while still regarding him as a barbarian, he was one of the first to sense that Shakespeare was a genius. Instead of drawing his inspiration solely from the ancient Greeks and Romans, he went for the subjects of his twenty-seven tragedies to far-away countries such as China, Peru and Babylon, or into French history. He did not shrink from violent action and pathos on the stage, nor from horror, crowd scenes and *coups de théâtre*. In short, the classical mould became increasingly, in his best plays, a moth-eaten outer garment which only impeded the action but did not really conceal an entirely novel theatrical reality. Is this why the modern reader is bored and put off? Whatever the explanation, whole blocks of the dramatic edifice have crumbled away. His comedies – in verse as the classical connexion required – are as neglected as his tragedies. The epic poet, the official poet, who strayed for a time (1745–7) into Louis xv's court, the author of the *Ducelle*, another epic poem but this one playful and scandalous, the ingenious composer of so many poems, epistles and tales in verse which delighted the century – all that remains of this impressive achievement is a handful of passages preserved in anthologies. His work in verse has simply not survived.

For the twentieth century, it is Voltaire's prose writings that count. In these he is not out to say something well, but just to say something. Even in his verse, despite the pointless constraint of rhyme, rhythm and the conventional eloquence, what he is usually seeking to convey to his reader is a series of moral and philosophical truths. If in his seven *Discours sur l'homme* (1734–7) there is not overmuch poetry, there is a great deal of psychological analysis and appreciation of ideas. He sometimes uses his plays, too, as a platform – which would have been unthinkable in the seventeenth century. His *Mahomet,* which he had the brilliant idea of dedicating to the Pope (1745), is a scathing attack on fanaticism. But there is no doubt that prose, especially from such an incisive and free-flowing pen, was a more direct vehicle for his thoughts. More and more as the years go by, it is in prose (and bypassing the faded literary genres) that he hammers home the messages closest to his heart.

These messages are few in number and they avoid profundity. Voltaire had no vaulting ambitions as a thinker. For him, pure speculation had little appeal. What he wants is action. He is tempted to dismiss contemplation as just one of the many forms of sloth. Pascal had dwelt on man's horror at 'remaining alone with himself', and on our misfortune when 'we see no one but ourselves'[96]. This is how Voltaire answers him in the twenty-fifth of his *Philosophical Letters* (1734): 'This expression "see no one but ourselves" is meaningless. What sort of man would it be who never acts and who is supposed simply to contemplate himself? I declare that such a man is not only an imbecile and a burden to society but that he cannot possibly exist. For what is he going to contemplate?'. In fact, man does not just think. He always thinks of *something*. 'It is impossible for human nature to persist in this imaginary sluggishness. Man is born for action, just as fire tends to rise and a stone to fall. For man not to be busy is not to exist'[97]. Our incapacity to know our essence, the meaning of life or of the life to come, to attain certainty, to solve our metaphysical or theological problems, all this should not discourage us. 'What man in his senses would try to hang himself because he does not know what God is like face to face, and because his reason cannot fathom the mystery of the Trinity? You might just as well despair at not having four feet and two wings'[98]. Wisdom consists in accepting your limitations as set by your nature. After all, 'of all animals, man is the most perfect, the happiest and the longest lived. It calls for a good deal of pride and temerity to claim [as do the dogmas of Original Sin and of the Fall] that we should be better than our nature makes us'[99]. Wisdom consists in being satisfied with such intelligence as we have, which is quite sufficient to bring a little more reasonableness, a little more happiness into our life on earth.

Religious fanaticism, he believes, is largely responsible for the woes

LE DÉJEÛNÉ DE FERNEY.

afflicting human society. 'There is hardly a town or village in Europe in which religious strife has not led to bloodshed'[100]. Revealed religions, Christianity in particular, are merely a collection of impostures which are firmly entrenched thanks to the impudence of some and the blindness of others. 'Jesus', he writes, 'is obviously a country bumpkin from Judea, no doubt a shade brighter than the other yokels in his part of the world. Without apparently being able to read or write, he set about creating a small sect, etc'[101]. As for God, we may read in the *Sermon des Cinquante* (1749) that he certainly 'cannot have been born of a maid or died on the gallows or been eaten in a piece of dough or have inspired these books [the Old and New Testaments] which swarm with contradictions, folly and horror'[102]. On every possible occasion, whatever the medium and the approach, he pours copious ridicule on the dogmas of Christianity and demolishes its base, sapping the power and authority of the church and combating the role and the very existence of the clergy.

(who for thirty years declared he was dying) is
surrounded by friends, including his niece,
Madame Denis, whose hand he is holding. On
the wall is the famous picture of the Calas family.
(Engraving by Nee after Denon, 1775.)

Voltaire was not content with general denunciations. He inter-
vened directly in a number of particularly revolting cases of intolerance. In 1762 a young Protestant called Calas committed suicide
at Toulouse. The whole family was imprisoned, and the boy's old
father, accused of having hanged his son for intending to become
Catholic, was condemned to death and executed. It was largely
thanks to Voltaire that the sentence of the Toulouse *Parlement*
was quashed and that Calas was finally rehabilitated in 1765. This
courageous campaign greatly enhanced the reputation of the
philosophe, and many of his contemporaries ranked the man of
action above the man of letters. '*Mahomet* is a sublime tragedy',
exclaims the interlocutor of Rameau's nephew (in Diderot's work),
'but I would rather have rehabilitated Calas'[103]. On the ruins of
fanaticism, Voltaire sees the dawn, if not of mutual comprehension,
at least of the acceptance of man by man, that is, of tolerance. And
indeed from that time on there was to be a little more humanity in
this cruel world. In a *Prière à Dieu* which he placed towards the end
of his reverberating *Treatise on Tolerance* (1763), Voltaire expresses
the wish 'that all these petty shades òf belief which distinguish one
of the atoms called men from the other should not be the signal for
hatred and persecution'. And he adds, 'May all men remember
that they are brothers! May they have a horror of tyranny over the
soul, as they execrate the brigandage that uses its might to seize
upon the fruit of labour and peaceful industry!'[104] We know that this
wish was to be granted a quarter of a century later, if not in fact then
at least on the statute book. The *Declaration of the Rights of Man*
in 1789 stipulates in its Article 10 that 'No one may be harassed for
his opinions, even if they are opinions on religious matters'. Voltaire's
sixty years of struggle had not been in vain.

The *Prière* referred to above is neither a figure of speech nor a
piece of deception. Voltaire's violent anti-clericalism, his militant
anti-Christianity and altogether his unceasing denunciation of dog-

matic religion must on no account be confused with irreligion or atheism. The author of *L'Athée et le Sage* (1775) was a believer in natural religion. He was profoundly convinced of the existence of a 'Supreme Being, necessary and incomprehensible, who created us'[105]. In this 'Being that has existed in itself from all eternity', he recognised the Newtonian God, the creator and guarantor of the law of attraction, a God who is a clockmaker, a geometrician and a mechanic, the architect of the universe and guardian of the laws instituted by Him. This great Being, whom all religions obscurely adore despite their outward differences, would never stoop to intervening arbitrarily in human affairs. Sister Broadbottom's rejoicing is therefore meaningless. 'You know', she cries, 'how much I love my sparrow. He would have died had I not said nine Ave Marias to obtain his recovery. God has brought my sparrow back to life.' To this a metaphysician, with a striking resemblance to Voltaire, retorts 'I don't think God is much concerned about your sparrow, however pretty it may be. Pray reflect, He has other matters on his mind. His immutable laws and his eternal immanence move the whole of nature. If your Ave Marias could prolong the life of Sister Broadbottom's sparrow for a single instant beyond the allotted span, these Ave Marias would have violated every law laid down from all eternity by the Supreme Being. You would have thrown the universe out of gear. You would have made it necessary to create a new world, a new God, a new order of things'[106]. The endorsement of scientific determinism thus comes full circle back to the feeling of human impotence – and even perhaps a certain fatalism[107].

This rather depressing deism is of a piece with the rather sombre vision of *Le monde comme il va* (1746). The spirit Ituriel weighs the positive and negative sides of Babouc's report on the town of Persepolis and comes to the following conclusion: 'Everything may not be good, but everything is tolerable'. In fact Babouc was very indulgent, for Voltaire over the years had become more and more acutely conscious of the imperfections and limitations of man's estate. He was profoundly affected by sudden death, with the loss (in 1749) of Madame du Châtelet, and by natural disasters such as the Lisbon earthquake of 1755, which in a matter of minutes destroyed a flourishing capital. The characters of *Candide ou L'Optimisme* (1759) come up against every possible manifestation of physical or moral evil in the course of their incessant peregrinations. To instance only self moral evil, the wretched Anabaptist Martin points out to Candide, who has given him shelter: 'On this globe, or rather on this globule . . . I have hardly ever seen a town which did not desire the ruin of its neighbour, or a family which did not desire to exterminate some other family. Everywhere the weak loathe the mighty before whom they crawl, and the mighty treat them like sheep whose only function is to provide meat and wool for sale. A million assassins in military formation rampage through Europe from one end to the other and use murder and robbery, executed with perfect discipline, to earn a living'[108]. And if, by good luck, man is left in peace, he is hardly any better off, for he is 'born to live in the convulsions of unquiet or in the lethargy of boredom'[109].

Such a description of man's estate brings to mind Pascal. Voltaire takes 'humanity's side' against the 'sublime misanthropist'[110] (as he called him), and reproaches him with seeking 'to horrify us with ourselves'. 'Men', he affirms, 'are as happy as human nature permits'[111]. He himself was always firmly resolved to take his full share of the physical, intellectual and artistic joys lavished on him by nature and civilisation. And he is not far from proclaiming this hedonism as a guiding principle,

> J'aime le luxe, et même la mollesse,
> Tous les plaisirs, les arts de toute espèce.[112]
>
> (Luxury I love, and even indolence;
> All pleasures, art of every kind.)

Candide is driven from the chateau – the paradise where he had been brought up – for having been caught behind a screen with the lovely Cunégonde: his wanderings through the wide world must now begin. Moreau le Jeune does not show in his engraving the 'grands coups de pied dans le derriere' mentioned by Voltaire. (Engraving of 1787 for the *Oeuvres complètes*.)

He appreciates painting, the opera, comfort, good cooking – everything that properly organised industry and commerce can provide for an opulent city. For him, civilisation is not just an empty word, and asceticism, whether of the Christian or Spartan brand, is simply absurd. Material progress, the development of the arts, the dissemination of enlightenment, have made man happier and better. Of this he is deeply convinced, and in this conviction his outlook is modern. In a moment of euphoria, he goes so far as to declare

Le Paradis terrestre est où je suis. [113]

(And Paradise on earth is where I am.)

In reality there is nothing to prevent man from creating this paradise for himself, but for the most part, as we have seen, it has still to be constructed. There is still an immense gap between man as he is, a prey to superstition, fanaticism, war and oppression, and man as he might be, free, happy, and enlightened – depending of course on his circumstances. It was in an effort to bridge this gap that Voltaire battled all his life.

He battled above all against ignorance – by spreading truth, by educating his public, by providing information. He was profoundly convinced, like Plato, that men usually act badly because they know not what they do. We must therefore rid them of their prejudices and mistaken beliefs. Voltaire threw himself ardently into the task. His whole work is a gigantic debunking campaign. In every field he lays bare absurdities and exposes them in their ridiculous, odious, intolerable reality. Thus little by little, washing away one layer after the other, he allows a rational human pattern of society to emerge, stripped of fanaticism and misguided ideas, a well-run society in which justice ceases to be meaningless. Is it really possible, once the utter scandalousness of the abuse has been grasped, to go on accepting (for example) the arbitrary reign of customary law? 'We have no laws . . . We are usually guided by custom. As each custom

Le Baron....voyant cette cause & cet effet, chassa Candide
du Château à grands coups de pied dans le derriere;

Candide Chap. 1.er

has inevitably gone on evolving in all of the provinces, like dress and headgear, judges can safely be guided by their caprice in choosing the practice that was in vogue four centuries back or the one that held good a year ago. This is a useful device for all dishonest litigants, and could not be more to the liking of judges, who with a clear conscience can judge the case without ever having understood it'[114]. And what of the use of torture in interrogating the accused? 'It is an infallible secret for saving those endowed with robust muscles'[115]. The reforms which did away with these abuses were to be the work, not of a people in revolt – that possibility did not occur to Voltaire – but of enlightened rulers such as Frederick the Great of Prussia or Catherine ii of Russia. However, for such reforms to become possible and even necessary, public opinion had to be pre-pared for them and welcome them unreservedly. They presuppose a transformation in the mentality of the age.

To study the mentality of the past, and at the same time the way of life corresponding to it, is the object of history. Voltaire made a notable contribution to its foundations as a humane science. As he points out at the beginning of his *Siècle de Louis XIV* (1751), 'it is not one man's deeds but all men's minds'[116] at work in the century which he sets out to depict. The book itself was presented, as early as 1756, as falling within the scope of a still vaster survey, *L'Essai sur l'Histoire générale et sur les Moeurs et l'Esprit des Nations depuis Charlemagne jusqu' à nos jours.* 'After reading three or four thousand descriptions of battles and the contents of a few hundred treaties', he observes, 'I found that I was hardly any better informed as regards the substance. All I learned from them was the bare facts'[117]. History, as he conceived it, is quite a different matter. It is history which 'sets peoples' rights before their eyes, and the events that concern a whole nation, their treaties with neighbouring nations, the progress of the useful arts, the abuses which constantly expose the majority to the tyranny of a tiny minority'[118]. *The History of Charles*

XII, King of Sweden (1751) remains a model of historical narration which reads like a novel and sometimes like an epic. *Le Siècle de Louis XIV,* despite a certain dispersal of the material over the various chapters, likewise remains the richest and most evocative storehouse of information of this sumptuous age. But Voltaire's main aim as a historian was to gauge the level of civilisation, to highlight the real values, to trace the path of enlightenment through the dark ages and to underline the extent of human progress. History did not divert him from the battle waged by the *philosophes*. It provided him with a basis for action, and set the struggle for progress in the perspective of the philosophy of history.

He deliberately discarded the traditional diction of polemics with its long, resounding periods. He took to using short, quick-fire sentences: 'It seems desirable to write nothing but what is simple, concise and intelligible to the most unsophisticated minds'[119]. He distrusted abstract reasoning, and relied on examples from real life which struck the imagination. He loathed portentous, dogmatic and systematic exposés and confined himself to illustrating specific truths. He almost always adopted the indirect approach. Instead of coming straight out with his conclusions, he allowed the reader the facile pleasure of piercing the transparent veil of fiction or irony. He naturally was at pains to be as varied as possible when he repeated himself. And he was unfailingly amusing.

Thus he gradually moved away from the traditional literary genres as well as from the usual forms of controversy towards other means of expressing his views which were better suited to his cast of mind and his need. This is where he scored his greatest triumphs. What sometimes struck his contemporaries as the demented buffoonery of a polemist who had lost all sense of reality is often what appears to a modern reader as the cream of his wit. During the last twenty-five or thirty years of his life in particular he poured out a stream of brochures and booklets which he published anonymously or under a pseudonym, attributing his writings to a whole gamut of the most improbable authors – letters, tales, dialogues, pronouncements, sermons, speeches, conversations, reports, harangues for the defence in which, be it parody or satire, there unfold before our eyes, in a flow of wildly absurd inventions, the follies of the world with all their trail of problems. There is the *Dialogue between a Brahman and a Jesuit* (1756) in which the former explains to the latter how, one fine day. he took it into his head 'to begin a little walk on the Malabar coast with the left foot first instead of the right one. And from that decision – obviously – there followed the death of Henri IV'[120]. There is the *Account of the Death of the Jesuit Berthier* (1759), poisoned by the fumes of two dozen copies of the *Journal de Trévoux,* a boring periodical of which he was the editor. Even a page of the *Encyclopédie* dipped in white wine which he is made to swallow cannot save him. There is the *Dialogue between the Capon and the Fowl* (1763) who exchange notes on their respective mutilations and on the sad fate to which they are condemned by those human bipeds, who, says the capon, 'are far beneath us since they have no feathers at all'[121]. Then there is *On the horrible Danger of Reading* (1765) in which the mufti Joussouf-Cheribi anathematises 'the diabolical invention of printing' for 'that means of communicating thoughts evidently tends to dissipate ignorance – the guardian and bulwark of well-policed states'[122].

There are above all the *Tales* which are today regarded as his masterpiece. In these, in a sobering series of comparisons, he whisks his two-dimensional characters from one end of the planet to the other, and subjects them to a frantic succession of the absurdities, horrors and catastrophes which are humanity's lot. The perfunctorily sketched picturesque setting, the swinging gaiety of the action. the improbable and intriguing twists of the story shed a poetic and lighthearted charm over these fragile and irridescent trifles. Never has human wretchedness been unfolded before us with such a

nimble and heady joyousness. The contrast is all the greater between the slight intoxication by which the reader is carried away and
the sombre lessons driven home by the tales. In *Candide*, Voltaire, by
the concrete situations in which he places his characters, denounces
or illustrates in turn caste prejudices, the folly of war, illnesses,
natural calamities and the Inquisition, etc., while all the time dwel-
ling on the further aberration whereby, faced with the haunting
spectacle of physical and moral evil, some people go on repeating
that 'all is well'.

The message preached by Voltaire is at its most effective in these
works, and the literary pleasure itself makes the reader more vul-
nerable to the propaganda. For him this carnival presided over by
reason is the most delightful of games by which to cut through to
the truth, hinted at beneath the flimsiest of disguises. The tone is so
right, the technique so simple, the wit so effervescent, exploding in
every line in preposterous sallies and dazzling shock effects as to
make of these wry pocket-size skits both artistic gems and heavy
ideological artillery. The tale is so enchanting that the reader swallows
the polemical medicine without realising it.

Voltaire is out to amuse, and he has a horror of bores. Many of
his readers have never forgiven him on that account. In the nineteenth century, Musset talks of his 'hideous smile'[123] and Joseph de
Maistre refers to his 'frightful sneer'[124]. The truth is quite different.
Voltaire's smile certainly does not betray the smug complacency of
Pangloss in *Candide* who maintains that all is for the best in the
best of all possible worlds. But neither does it express the unhealthy
Schadenfreude of the destructive intelligence at mankind's ruinous
plight which it would be overjoyed to enumerate in detail. That
smile denotes the superiority of the mind which stigmatises the
shackles of necessity and uses laughter, in a way, as a means of
obtaining its liberty (which is in effect humour). Evil is often ridiculous. To laugh at evil does not mean to do away with it, but at

least to loosen its hold and restrict its sway, put some distance between us and it and to gird up our loins to fight it when there is some point in doing so. Voltaire's laugh is good for morale. It trounces the enemy. It is a propedeutic of humanist action.

However, since the romantics in particular we have a distressing tendency to imagine that the boring or the obscure is necessarily linked with the profound. Voltaire, who tries to be clarity itself, has suffered from this absurd prejudice. Baudelaire, admittedly in hasty jottings which he would not have though of publishing, assures us that 'Voltaire, like all idlers, hated mystery' and denounces him as 'the king of chatterboxes, the prince of superficial minds, . . . the porters' preacher'[125]. Nothing could be more unfair. Voltaire does not deny the existence of mystery. He circumscribes it. And if he turns his back on it as much as possible, it is because he is incapable of whiling his life away with his gaze fixed on the Unknowable, and he responds to the urge of action. What he can be reproached with is his inability to stay quiet in a room, it is his turbulence and his restlessness, not his laziness. In the same way, he is far from being superficial. He intentionally restricts his field and his focus. He is hardly a philosopher in the present meaning of the term, and he distrusts theological and metaphysical speculation. But, in the territory in which he takes his stand and which is broadly speaking that of man as a social being, what perceptiveness, what penetration he displays!

Of course, he did not construct a system or even a doctrine. One is struck, perhaps disappointed, by the fact that this prodigious work is largely a patchwork of fragments, an aggregate in which there is no pattern. The thinker is soon out of breath, and his ideas peter out after a few pages. It would seem that he constantly practised the Cartesian precept of 'dividing the difficulties into . . . as many parts as possible and as would be needed to arrive at the best solution'[126], but retained his distrust of conclusions and syntheses. It is therefore in compendia that he finds his ideal vehicle. One system of presentation which is clear and not open to discussion is the alphabetical order. It is significant that he often falls back on it. He composed a repertory of opinions on that basis, and in 1764 he published the admirable *Portable Philosophical Dictionary,* one of his most varied and richest works. Elsewhere he made long lists of problems which he then treated one by one. In a few pages, he enumerated the sixty-six scandalous questions of the fictitious Zapata, Professor of Theology at Salamanca (1767) or, in nine volumes, he examined the *Questions on the Encyclopédie* (1770–2). In all these cases, what he offers the reader is a series of self-contained passages which in their totality give the impression of a broken mirror, in which the same handful of propositions are reflected over and over again. The ardent propagandist hand in hand with the pedagogue and his unwearying repetitions definitely takes pride of place over the thinker.

What has survived of Voltaire is mainly his wit and the cast of his mind. His wit sparkles. It radiates fantasy, irony and humour in all his works and all through his endless *Correspondence* in which Voltaire the man can be seen at his tasks. His mentality consists in never allowing himself to be duped, in demanding the right to take everything to pieces, in refusing to submit to orthodoxy of any kind, in denouncing all the abuses which weigh mankind down, in the joyous exercise of his intelligence. He is one of the men who inspired the liberal movement of the nineteenth century, but Monsieur Homais, the smug chemist in Flaubert's *Madame Bovary,* is only a caricature of that trend. He is Voltairean in much the same way as the Salvation Army is Rousseauist. Whatever one may say, the Voltairean spirit is in no way linked to an outdated capitalism. The distrust of verbiage, the passion for lucidity, the horror of fanaticism, and of the dogmatic creeds from which it springs – all these virtues are highly relevant to the life of the present time.

L'accordée de village by Greuze. Diderot discussed this painting in detail in his *Salon* of 1761. What delighted him above all was the moving quality in this scene of family life (the signing of the marriage contract) and the truth of the artist's observation. Musée du Louvre.

Diderot

Of all the eighteenth-century *philosophes,* Diderot is probably the closest to the modern mind[127]. For his contemporaries he was first and foremost the man who directed the *Encyclopédie.* But, despite this militant role which put him in the forefront of the intellectual scene, some of his features were still in shadow. In fact, for reasons which are still somewhat mysterious, he did not think it opportune to publish those of his works which to our way of thinking are the richest and most profound. When he died in 1784 such fundamental writings as *Le Neveu de Rameau, Jacques le Fataliste, La Religieuse, Le Paradoxe sur le comédien* and *Le Rêve de D'Alembert* were still in manuscript. They were only to see the light of day from 1796 on, and an important part of his scintillating correspondence was not made public till the twentieth century. In any case, certain aspects of such a highly original creation were utterly beyond his contemporaries. The significance of his materialistic views and his biological hypotheses has not been fully grasped till the last fifty years. The implications of his experiments with the novel were only recently realised. More light has perhaps been shed on his work than on that of any other author by the research and inquiring mind characteristic of our age. His writings have taken on a new dimension.

The production of the *Encyclopédie,* which had originally been merely a publishing venture, satisfied Diderot's fundamental needs. It was in line with his frenzied, universal curiosity. As the needs of the case and alphabetic order dictated, he composed or knocked into shape articles on the techniques of various crafts, the natural sciences, the methodology and philosophy of science, the history of philosophy, law, political philosophy, language and so on. While passionately interested in specific details, and particularly in discoveries in what is now defined as biology, he went on from there

to ponder on the basis of knowledge, on its elaboration, its pattern, its division into separate and complementary sciences. For a quarter of a century, the direction of this immense survey propelled him, in a ceaseless intellectual ferment, into the concrete problems posed by the organisation and methodology of ideas, frequently parallelled by the difficulties arising from human relations with the members of the team. There can be no more varied discipline or one better calculated to exercise the intellectual muscles and enrich the mind. It is almost enough to explain his characteristic agility, were it not obviously his inborn flexibility that fitted him for the work and enabled him to follow the twists and turns of his collaborators' thought and to give faithful expression to it. If that work can be said to reflect a particular spirit, it is a modern scientific spirit which has 'the general interest of mankind at heart'[128], a reforming progressive spirit – in short, the Enlightenment. Yet the *Encyclopédie* does not strictly speaking propound a doctrine. This is hardly sur-

prising in view of the latitude left to the authors and the compart-
mentalisation of the subject matter.

As against this, Diderot's own general orientation is clear
enough. A rationalist, a sensualist, a determinist, he comes close to
monist materialism. The conclusions drawn by him from scientific
progress are much more radical than those of most of his contemporaries. In 1746, aged almost thirty-three, he recalls in his *Philosophical Thoughts* that 'matter has existed from all eternity, and that
movement is essential to it'. That being so, 'given the infinite range
of possible combinations'[129], the present structure of the universe,
he suggests, may very well have been the work of chance. The book
was promptly condemned, and in 1749 the audacity of *Letters on
the Blind* was patent enough to earn him three months' confinement
in the dungeon of Vincennes. His *Essay on the Interpretation of
Nature* (1753–4) ends with a string of questions such as this: 'How
can matter not be one, and either all living or all dead? Is living
matter always living? And is dead matter always dead? Does living
matter not die? Does dead matter never come alive?' And this outline of materialism is already tinged with transformism and even
evolutionism. May we not, wonders the *philosophe,* go so far as to
'suspect that, from all eternity, the animal kingdom's own elements
were scattered throughout matter and mingling with it, that these
elements happened to unite, because this was possible, that the
embryo formed by these elements passed through an infinite number
of stages of organisation and development, that it successively ac-
quired movement, sensation, ideas, thought, reflection, consciousness, feelings, passions, signs, gestures, sounds, articulate sounds,
language, laws, the sciences and arts, that millions of years elapsed
between each of these developments, that matter may be subject to
other developments and be capable of further growth still unknown
to us?' Some of the major themes of Diderot's thought are already
present in these questions. He was to return to them again and again

throughout his life. He adds, as he was bound to do, that 'religion saves us from many a slip and considerable effort' by teaching us 'that the animals issued from the hands of the Creator as they are today'[130]. But nobody was deceived by this precaution.

He is even more explicit in some writings composed in 1769, so explicit that he did not risk publishing them – *L'entretien entre D'Alembert et Diderot* and *Le Rêve de D'Alembert*. There is, he assures us, no break between the mineral and the animal series or between minerals and animals. Marble is edible. A man can live perfectly well on vegetables sown on land into which marble powder has been mixed. There is therefore a transition 'from marble to humus, from humus to the vegetable kingdom, and from the vegetable kingdom to the animal kingdom, that is, to flesh'[131]. The chain of living things is continuous and 'all beings live and move within each other'[132]. D'Alembert exclaims in his dream 'Every animal is to some extent a man; every mineral is to some extent a plant; every plant is to some extent an animal'. As early as 1765 Diderot affirmed that 'sensation is a universal property of matter – inert in an inanimate body, active in such a body thanks to the assimilation of a living animal substance'[133]. Matter is composed entirely of molecules which determine in their aggregate and temporary structure what we call life and consciousness. The soul itself is matter, for 'it is hard to admit that somewhere a being can exist which yet does not correspond to any point in space'[134]. Besides we ourselves know in a way from experience the identity of body and soul. A propos of one of his characters, Diderot observes 'The distinction between a physical world and a moral one seemed to him meaningless'[135]. And matter is eternal: 'To be born, to live and to pass on is to change one's form. Alive, I act and react as a mass. Dead, I act and react as a group of molecules'[136]. He had launched the same idea in much the same words in 1759 when, writing to his friend Sophie Volland, he reported a conversation which he had just had with an elderly man: 'The only difference I know between life and death,' he had said, 'is that at present you live in a mass, and that when you are dissolved and dispersed into molecules twenty years from now, you will be living in tiny fragments'[137].

These grandiose vistas, the scientific fruitfulness of which has since been so amply demonstrated, are put forward as lyrical hypotheses in a sort of poetic fervour. His friend Grimm is right to see in him 'a man inspired, driven forward by the daemon of light and truth'[138]. The first consequence which he draws for Mademoiselle Volland from the theory which he has just expounded to her is that 'those who have loved each other during their life and who arrange to be buried side by side are not perhaps as mad as people might think. Perhaps their ashes press against each other, mingle and unite. Indeed, they have perhaps not lost all feeling, all recollection of their original state. O my dear Sophie, let me cling to this fancy, this dear fancy! It would give me the assurance of eternity within you and with you'[139]. This sentimental effusion, it will be seen, flows effortlessly from scientific conjecture. The thinker is also the man of feeling, just as he is the philanthropist and lover of virtue. The lucidity and the cynicism of this materialism may rule out illusion, but not bursts of feeling. While subscribing to this biophysical determinism, which might have stifled his elation, he gives himself up unrestrainedly to the cult of sentiment current at the time.

He bears a close resemblance to one of his heroes – Jacques the Fatalist who, he writes, 'did not know the meaning of the word vice or that of virtue [and] believed that man gravitated towards glory or ignominy as inevitably as a ball (if endowed with consciousness) rolls down a mountainside . . . In the light of this system it might be imagined that Jacques was never delighted or grieved by anything at all. However, this was not so. He behaved much as you or I would do. He thanked anyone who did him a good turn; he flew into a rage over injustice'[140]. In the same way, instead of regarding vice and virtue as two separate facets of human nature (just as clay and granite are two geological varieties), Diderot detests vice while virtue affords him unspeakable pleasure. 'The sight of injustice', he confides to his friends, 'moves me to such a burst of indignation that I am out of my mind . . . but the sight of equitable deeds fills me with such sweetness, inflames me with such a glow, such a rapture, that, even if I had to lose my life, I would not care'[141]. It is this transport of sentiment which he tries to provoke by introducing so many moving situations in his two *drames bourgeois* (middle-class dramas) – the *Fils naturel* (1757) and *Le Père de Famille* (1760). It is the same pitch of emotion that is inspired in him by Greuze's pictures and utilised as one of the main ingredients of art criticism in his nine *Salons* (from 1759 to 1781). He writes à propos of Greuze's composition *The Paralytic:* 'When I saw this eloquent, moving old man, I felt . . . my soul melting and the tears ready to fall'[142]. But it is no easy task to reconcile the message of the feelings and the scientific approach. The free and enthusiastic acceptance of spontaneous charity by the virtuous man hardly seems compatible with the strict profession of a determinism that is more or less fatalistic. Diderot is fully aware of this difficulty, for he confesses to Sophie 'It is hard to abandon oneself blindly to the universal torrent . . . If I believe that I love you of my own free will, I am mistaken. My love for you is nothing of the kind. O, what a wonderful system for ingrates! I am furious at being entangled in this damned philosophy which my mind cannot help approving and my heart denying'[143].

But are the Beautiful and the Good really linked in one and the same feeling? No, for after all if this feeling is 'the hall-mark of goodness of heart', it is also typical 'of the mediocrity of genius'[144]. The famous *Paradoxe sur le comédien* proves that the great actor is a cool, intelligent observer who is devoid of feeling and whose attitudes and movements are carefully calculated. 'The gestures of his despair are taken from memory; they were thought out in front

of a mirror'[145]. When he sheds tears, 'they make their way down
from the brain' instead of rising from the heart[146]. This is what
explains his self-control and the evenness of his theatrical effects
from one performance to the next. The impression of reality which
he achieves is a very specific one – stage reality, which is very different from that of life. 'Great poets, like great actors, are the most
unfeeling of men.' Moreover, 'feeling is hardly what makes a great
genius . . . It is not his heart, it is his head that does everything'[147].
Artistic creation has rarely been interpreted in such radically intellectual terms. A dozen years earlier Diderot seemed to subscribe
to an entirely different conception. He dwelt on the warmth, the
capacity for enthusiasm which seems to characterise genius, and
showed the poet inspired by the pre-romanticism of the darkness of
night, the storm, the tempest, the depths of the forest and ruins.
'Poetry', he adds, 'calls for something vast, barbaric and wild'[148].
There is strictly speaking nothing incompatible between the poet
in the grip of enthusiasm and the calculating actor. With both,
artistic creation presupposes the same 'spirit of observation', the
same direct intuition of the means needed for it to take effect, the
same power of divination which he calls the 'prophetic spirit'[149].
But their intellectual atmosphere is utterly different. 'Is man then
condemned to be at loggerheads both with his fellowmen and with
himself on the only matters which he desperately seeks to know –
truth, goodness and beauty?'[150]

Yet Diderot is never a prisoner of this relativistic and sceptical
subjectivism which in any case goes against the grain of his character.
He immediately puts it behind him by a series of clear affirmations.
But it would be a gross error to try to freeze a man who is as mer-
curial as life and conversation in the artificial conflict between
spontaneity and reflection, or between heart and mind – or for that
matter in any philosophical position whatsoever. True, he is well
aware and sometimes uneasily so – that his imagination, his reason

and his feelings are pulling him in different directions. But if his consciousness is divided, it cannot be said that it is torn in two, for he really has no settled doctrines. Always evolving, always in action, his thought refuses to be crystallised into a system. The moment of summing up, of synthesis, never comes. Unceasingly his mind calls everything in question, including itself. It could not stop seeking for itself or fleeing from itself without ceasing to exist. The essence of its continuity lies in its dynamism, not in its ideas. It comes to terms with itself, consolidates its position, then bounces back into the mêlée with its diversity, its disparities and its contradictions. It all reminds one of Jacques the Fatalist who 'was inconsistent like you and me and who tended to forget his principles, except in certain circumstances when his principles obviously kept their hold on him'[151]. What we have here, then, is an everyday and sometimes visceral philosophy which it is difficult to keep apart from the *philosophe* himself, whose overpowering personality and whose capricious verve and moods it expresses[152]. The epigraph of *Le Neveu de Rameau* appositely recalls Vertumnus, that mutable god of the Romans who presided over changes in the weather. He is truly the God of Diderot as well. To compose his face in an expression is to betray him. On being shown the fine portrait painted of him by Van Loo in 1767, he exclaimed 'This is not me. In a single day I had a hundred different expressions, depending on what affected me at the time. I was serene, sad, dreamy, tender, violent, passionate, elated'[153]. Diderot's real physiognomy therefore is to be sought in the multiple facets of daily life, in the totality of individual instants which are wonderfully recreated in a living unity by the duration of the living word. Diderot's philosophy would hardly be more than a rather cold, gaunt ideology if it were not generated by a writer and an artist with the knack of preserving ideas in all their pristine freshness. In fact he clothes the ideas in flesh and blood; he brings them alive and tries them out in a literary

universe, a profoundly original and captivating literary universe.

If he wishes to launch a particularly daring hypothesis in which the scientific imagination borders on poetic frenzy, he uses as his mouthpiece a sleep-talker, and notes down the man's confused babblings. This is *Le Rêve de D'Alembert*. Addressing himself to Sophie Volland, Diderot shows that he is perfectly conscious of the means needed to achieve certain ends: 'This is utterly fantastic and at the same time profoundly philosophical. There is no little skill involved in putting my ideas in the mouth of a dreamer. One must often clothe wisdom in the garb of madness in order to secure acceptance for it'[154]. It is, in a way, the hypothetical expression of a hypothesis. Language and literary technique in Diderot are quite inseparable from the thought. We need only take a closer look at the dialogue for

This portrait by Van Loo of Diderot appeared in the *Salon*
of 1767, where he commented: 'Very alive. Catches
the sitter's gentleness and his vitality. But too young,
the head too small. A feminine prettiness, ogling,
smiling, delicate fastidious, pouting . . . The look of a
Secretary of State, not of a philosopher . . . It is not me.'

215

which he has such a marked predilection that it often crops up even in his letters. This form suits his way of thinking to perfection. The dialogue is not at all a sleight of hand designed to create an immediate 'living' effect. It is not a rhetorical technique but a philosophical instrument for experimenting with ideas.

That it is a flexible and unhampered experimentation is evident in *Le Neveu de Rameau,* undoubtedly the most scintillating and the most carefully worked over of his dialogues. Diderot himself comes on the stage right at the outset. We see him in his daily strolls in the Palais Royal: 'I talk to myself about politics, love, taste and philosophy'. It is this soliloquy which is to blossom into a dialogue when the *philosophe* settles down in the Café de la Régence, and strikes up a conversation with a quaint, picturesque and bohemian character – the nephew of the great composer Rameau. The ideas and problems on which Diderot ruminated all by himself are tried out on two personalities, *He* and *I,* the incarnation of two very different moral attitudes. With both of them, it should be added, the philosopher is familiar, which means of course that what we are really listening to is a dialogue between one *I* and another, or at least between two possible *I*'s. Vis-à-vis the *I* who is a partisan of reason and virtue, rather conventional by the way, the role reserved for *He* is to pin the other down with concrete proof of the impossibilities, the *aporia* of morals. This parasitic sensualist, unprincipled, ready to turn his hand to anything and pimp if occasion offers, has in fact the merit of lucidity and logic. 'One can profit', he notes, 'from bad company as from dissoluteness. One is compensated for the loss of one's innocence by the loss of one's prejudices'[155]. And in another passage he exclaims 'Do not press me, for I am very consistent'[156].

However, his attitude, shocking though it may be, can surely hardly be otherwise if transcendental values are denied and materialism is professed. In that case, wisdom apparently consists in 'drinking good wine, gorging oneself on delicate food and rolling in the hay with attractive women ... All the rest is vanity. – What, defend one's country? – Vanity. There is no fatherland any longer. From pole to pole all I see is tyrants and slaves. – Serve one's friends? – Vanity. Has one any friends? – A rank in society and the discharge of its function? – Vanity. What does it matter whether one has a station or not, provided one is rich, since the only reason for taking up a station is to become rich?'[157] These implacable rejoinders are interspersed with remarks in the rest of the book which are just as explosive, for example: 'Whatever one does, one cannot dishonour oneself if one is rich'[158]; 'The voice of conscience and honour is extremely weak when the bowels cry out'[159]; 'Rotting under marble or rotting under ground is still rotting'[160]; 'In nature, all species devour each other; all classes devour each other in society'[161]. And this world of forces and appetites is governed by determinism. Hence it is rather pointless to wonder whether things are not as they ought to be.

Against this radically despairing vision, *I* can find little else to set against it but 'the charms of virtue'[162]. But *He* can reply with some justification '[You] have ... on [your] side a sense which I lack, a fibre which has not been granted me'. We are harpsichords. 'Our senses are only so many strings which are plucked by nature around us, and which often pluck themselves'[163]. The *He* harpsichord lacks a string which the *I* harpsichord possesses. Their disaccord seems to flow from a difference in temperament. Besides, *I* and *He* agree on quite a number of points, as is clear from the text itself as well as from what we gather of Diderot's thought in his other works. Their experience and their diagnosis, if not their practice of social life, are fairly similar; if their actual behaviour is markedly different, their theories are often close to each other. In particular, they both expect their way of life to make them happy. Their hedonistic inclinations are the same, only their means differ.

These convergences are all the more disturbing as Diderot regards Rameau-*He* as a 'sluggard, a glutton, a coward, a filthy creature'[164].

In fact, in this dialogue between the virtuous materialist and the vicious materialist, *I* does not really try to set out his views. Apart from a few tirades, mainly on the joys of doing good, he is content to give *He* his cue. The focus is definitely on Rameau, as the title indicates. It is *his* personality and the related problems which constitute the central theme of the work. His passion for music, his whimsical character, his dazzling pantomimes, his impudent cynicism, his whole appearance correspond fairly closely to what we know of him from history. But Diderot has infused into him a good deal of his own personality, and, out of this café eccentric, out of this product of an ailing society, he has succeeded in creating a character at once fascinating and repugnant, a sort of anti-genius which takes a compelling hold of the reader. The psychological, literary and artistic brilliance of the portrait enriches and gives depth to the moral and philosophical meaning of the work. Diderot has the gift of clothing his ideas and problems in flesh and blood, in characters which continue to haunt us, so that they go on perpetually echoing in our mind. Far from being a mere ideological phantasy, highly ingenious no doubt but of no great importance, *Le Neveu* thrusts before us an irresistible reality which by its mere existence threatens to explode society and morals.

Diderot's greatness lies not only in the creativeness of his philosophy and his intuitions of genius, but also, and perhaps above all, in his skill at creating life. He has the seer's power of identifying himself with his characters, of getting under their skin, of thinking their thoughts, of speaking their language, and the artist provides the imaginative writer with means to move forward from a predominantly subjective and fleeting vision to a universal and lasting creation. One day he was sitting at his desk, when a friend 'called on him and found him in deep distress and his face bathed in tears.

"What's wrong? What a state you're in. What's wrong?". He re-
plied "I am upset at a tale I am telling myself ".[165]. These tears are
not the meaningless expression of a hypersensitive intellectual
spinning himself a yarn with too vivid a realisation of the phantoms
of his imagination. But they do denote an extraordinary degree of
participation by the writer in his characters' fate. At that time Diderot
was busy on *La Religieuse*. In the straight-forward account of the
adventures and sufferings of the wretched Suzanne Simonin, a nun
despite herself, he is clearly describing his own adventures and his
own sufferings. For he *is* Suzanne Simonin, while remaining the
artist Diderot, capable of transforming real facts into abiding
artistic, general truth, and thus enabling the nun to speak more
directly and more convincingly than she would herself. The same
ability to mould his material to perfection and the same mastery of
technique shine in his admirable *Tales*. The reader of these short
stories has the acute and disturbing feeling of hearing the exactly
right tone, and the unique, irreplaceable voice of each of the
characters.

A creativeness of this kind can hardly afford to be slapdash. In
his dialogue *Jacques le Fataliste et son maître,* Diderot admittedly
portrays a fatalist whose doctrine is shown as being at grips with
circumstances. But what is even more important is the way in which
the author delights in threading one story into the other, in showing
the sheer power of story-telling which confers existence on whatever
it names. As if to bring home to the reader the magical powers of
his art, he pauses maliciously, time and time again, to emphasise
that things could at any given point have followed an entirely different course. And in fact 'with a little imagination and talent for
style, nothing is easier than to concoct a novel'[166]. Now as it happens
Diderot does not write a novel – or rather, as in *Le Neveu* and *La
Religieuse,* he invents a new type of novel which looks forward to
the research and innovations of our time. 'Let us stay in the realm

of truth', he went on. It is not only Diderot's fantasy which governs the tales told by Jacques to his master during their endless wanderings around the world. Reality has a number of imperatives, for example as regards tone and facts, which it is impossible to disregard. This work in which the author seems to take every liberty, this haphazard dialogue conducted in unspecified conditions has its own rules and laws and operates within the framework of an exacting experiment with reality – and also in a new literary genre. What makes Diderot unique is that his addiction to ideology is not divorced from a sense of concrete detail. The thinker and the artist are indivisible.

Rousseau

With Jean-Jacques Rousseau[167] a new concept of literature appears on the scene. Book becomes inseparable from author. Its aim is still the aim of all *philosophe* literature – to spread ideas – but these ideas are so closely bound up with the personality of the man who writes and feels them that they cannot be understood unless we follow them back to the man within. At a time when so many works were published without their author's name, Rousseau signed all his, even *La Nouvelle Héloïse* (of which he pretended to be only the editor). But he was eager, he said in the preface, to answer for it. Behind that book, and behind the others, was a man who considered it as a deed for which he was always ready to assume responsibility. It is therefore natural and indeed essential to trace the work back to its author, in whom the ideas which it expounds are personified and reveal their true significance. Rousseau's own approach was no different. 'I never read a moral or philosophical work', he relates, 'without imagining that I beheld the soul and the principles of the man who wrote it. I regarded all these grave writers as modest men, wise, virtuous and irreproachable'[168]. He was soon undeceived, and 'this childish prejudice was dissipated'. But what was a mistake in the case of these philosophical charlatans becomes a valid rule where he is concerned. His books send the reader back to the writer, and they are to an increasing extent about him.

If in his first works he rarely talks about himself – the two *Discourses* of 1750 and 1755 afforded him scant opportunity to do so – from 1762 on, from the *Letters to M. de Malesherbes* to the *Rêveries du Promeneur Solitaire* via of course the autobiographical *Confessions* and the *Dialogues,* his work is one long self-revelation. The apologetic side is undoubtedly important. Rousseau, the persecuted nonconformist, defends himself against his detractors and accusers. But in fact he talks about himself and puts himself before the reader much more than he justifies himself. By going over his life again and by laying himself bare, he is pursuing the plan for moral education which he had always cherished. He continues to furnish, but directly from now on, the testimony of an exceptional yet typical man. Thus, the relations between the author and his public go beyond strictly intellectual contacts. They are characterised by an emotional tension and are analysed in terms of love and hate. In the end the book becomes for the reader a means, if he has the capacity, of communicating with a privileged being, of knowing and loving him. Carried to its logical extreme, the work would be swallowed up in the feeling to which it gives rise. For anyone who felt that he was Jean-Jacques' friend and brother would no longer have any need for his books, since by communing with his master he would be applying in his heart the essence of the teaching which far transcends any intellectual conversation.

Here we have the seeds of a religion, of the cult of Jean-Jacques or Rousseauism according to whether it is envisaged as a mystique or an ideology. Rousseau is not like the common run of writers. He declares vigorously 'I have always felt that an author's status could not be illustrious and respected except in so far as it was not a trade'[169], and continues, recalling in another passage the circumstances in which his first *Discourse* was composed, 'I found that I had become ... a man of letters precisely because I despised that status'[170]. Thus, paradoxically, he creates a literature founded on a hatred of literature and of literary men. Of the readers of this anti-literature who were to become friends, and almost devotees, Rousseau demands purity of heart. He expects them to measure up to his requirements as regards nature, training and nationality. 'I do not know two Frenchmen', he was to maintain, 'who could get to know me even if they so desired it with all their heart. The primitive nature of man is too far removed from their way of thinking'[171]. For this moral initiation, for this contact, a sort of grace is needed which is not vouchsafed to all. But for anyone possessing it, to read Rousseau is a devastating experience which should lead to conversion.

A complete and effective conversion, moreover, whereby one is swept into another universe in which great and hitherto unsuspected truths are revealed in every field – individual and social morality, theology, psychology, education, politics, economics and so on. The disciple – and this is a constant feature of Rousseau's teaching – must make the same pilgrimage as the Master. This conversion is in fact the one which Jean-Jacques himself underwent during his famous enlightenment in the summer of 1749, when he learnt of the question proposed by the Academy of Dijon: *Whether the Progress of the Sciences and the Arts has made for the Corruption or the Purification of Morals?* 'The very moment I read this question I saw a new world and I became a new man'[172] he recalls. The ideas on which we are living are wrong and harmful. 'I saw only error and madness in the doctrine of our sages, oppression and wretchedness in our social system'[173]. Rousseau at once became aware of his mission. 'I thought that I was made for the task of dissipating all this spurious glamour.' And in fact in all his works thereafter he

A popular engraving of the Ermitage where Rousseau stayed
between 1756 and 1757. 'I spent enchanting days by myself',
he wrote in his third letter to M. de Malesherbes,
'with only my good and simple housekeeper, my beloved dog,
my old cat, with the birds and the deer of the forest,
with nature and her ineffable creator'.

was to try and take the reader with him into this 'other intellectual
world whose simple and proud outline he [was unable] to contemplate without a feeling of enthusiasm'. For this revelation, it should
be noted, is that of a system and an order. The truths which he now
devoted his life to preaching are few in number, are interconnected
and form a coherent whole. For twenty years, with unflagging per-
sistence, he propounded, repeated, re-asserted and developed them
in each of his books. In 1762 he felt himself entitled to point out to
the Archbishop of Paris, who had let his previous works pass
without censuring them and who was now condemning *Emile*, 'I
have written on various subjects but I always expound the same
principles, the same morality, the same belief, the same maxims,
and, if you like, the same opinions'[174].

His basic idea is that of the goodness of nature, primitive purity
and the value of spontaneity. 'The first promptings of nature are
always the right ones . . . Man is naturally good[175]. If man is now
perverted and unhappy, this is because Society, its institutions and
laws have spoiled the simplicity of the earlier times. The progress of
knowledge and techniques, he replies to the Dijon Academy question, 'has added nothing to our real happiness . . . it has corrupted
our morals'[176]. It is obvious what a scandal such an assertion must
have made in an age when many were tempted to affirm that the
general level of morality was a function of the spread of knowledge
and to establish a close link between science, virtue and happiness.
Coming as he did halfway through the century, Rousseau exclaims
'All powerful God . . . deliver us from Light', and he denounces the
'hideous ravages to which the advent of the printing press has
already led in Europe'. He has really travelled into a new world.
Bernardin de Saint Pierre, an enthusiastic disciple, was to go so far
as to write on the *Pleasures of Ignorance*[177].

Man must forsake the towns and find himself again in the midst
of solitude. It is within himself and not in the pernicious teaching of

society life that he will find maxims to guide his action. 'We have an inner guide which is far more infallible than any book.'[178] Virtue is 'the sublime science of simple souls; ... Is it not enough to learn [its] laws, to listen to the promptings of the heart, and to the voice of conscience when the passions are still? This is real philosophy'[179]. Let us therefore lend an ear to the evidence of sentiment. If we are scrupulously faithful to the verities that well up in the depth of our being – to sincerity, that is – we shall safeguard ourselves against evil, if not against error. In any case, the material consequences of our actions are less important than the purity of our intentions. The main point is that we should allow our inborn goodness to speak out. But to find the natural man within us under the dross with which society has overlaid it, we must go back to the simple life, in harmony with nature, whether it be pastoral or wild, and blend with it. It is only in nature that we can joy in ourselves and abandon ourselves to the innocent delights of sentiment. Having then regained our unity, we shall find within ourselves, in the irresistible evidence of the heart and without recourse to churches or dogmas, the affirmation of the Supreme Being, a just and kind God. Thus redeemed and reconciled, we shall have carried out the reformation to which Jean-Jacques subjected himself in 1751 after his first *Discourse*. The only step remaining is to imbue society with this experience and these principles, since we cannot hope to put the clock back and the unsophisticated happiness of primitive times has been destroyed once and for all. But at least luxury must be proscribed, as must corrupting amusements. In fact, everything that diverts us from the simple life according to nature. And we must define the contract which constitutes society and guarantees the happiness of all.

A fair number of these topics are dealt with forcefully in the 1750 *Discourse* and in the 1755 *Discourse on the Origins and the Basis of Inequalities among Men*. In these two works which made him famous, a curious genius bursts upon us. It miraculously combines merits which are usually incompatible. On the one hand, Rousseau is a fantastic dialectician who can expound his subject matter with the same convincing clarity as his enemies, the *philosophes*. He deduces, he demonstrates, at times he quibbles. He organises his ideas with a fine logical sweep into architectural masses. He is as much at ease in hairsplitting over trifles as in painting a broad doctrinal fresco. He has a tough, confident mind, a sure touch and unflagging energy. On the other hand, even disregarding the rhetoric inseparable from a formal discourse, he has an eloquent turn of phrase. It has charm, plenitude, and harmony. Strangely enough, its transparency does not rule out music. In short, those who do not like Jean-Jacques see him as a rhetorician who makes words sing and at the same time as a sophist who juggles with ideas. But the rest are struck by this unusual combination in one man of a magician, a logician, a thinker and a poet.

Every page in the three great works published in swift succession in 1761 and 1762 is alive with these diverse talents. These are *La Nouvelle Héloïse,* the *Contrat Social* and *Emile.* Each of them has a complete literary originality, a tone, a rhythm which are peculiar to it. Yet they form a real trilogy which, in a clearly continuous *opus,* makes up a whole and has a particularly striking unity of purpose. It is the epic, now demonstrative, now lyrical, of the restoration of natural man.

This process must start at birth. *Emile* deals with the somewhat contradictory subject of his education. That, it might be imagined, would seek above all to be purely negative. We must learn to let nature have its way and learn how to listen to its voice. 'Observe nature and follow the path marked out by it'[180]. With an almost symbolic gesture, society almost strangles the newborn child as soon as it emerges from its mother's womb. Let us free it from these unnatural wrappings, its swaddling clothes. The general practice is to hand the child over to a nurse who is not specially concerned about it. Let us restore it to its natural nurse, its mother. Let us accustom it at once to simplicity. No luxurious rattles in gold or coral. 'A poppy head in which you can hear the sound of the seeds, a stick of liquorice which it can suck or chew will amuse it quite as much as these magnificent baubles'[181]. Besides, if it is at all possible, education should be in the country. 'A town is a bottomless pit swallowing up mankind . . . So send your children to draw new strength and to regain, among green fields, the vigour which they lose in the unhealthy air of overpopulated places'[182]. Immersed in nature, in contact with the elements, accustomed to open air and cold baths, the child will develop freely.

What kind of education should he be given? First of all what nature, through chance experience, lavishes on him spontaneously. Instead of a bookish approach to teaching, there should be lessons of and about things. It is only when the child is about twelve that we

On February 24 1776, Rousseau came to Nôtre Dame to place the manuscript of his *Dialogues* (Rousseau, juge de Jean-Jacques) on the high altar, with the inscription 'An offering entrusted to Providence'. He found the door to the choir shut and abandoned the idea. (Engraving after Le Barbier for *Oeuvres posthumes*, 1783.)

should venture 'to draw back the sacred curtain of nature'[183] and begin to initiate him into the sciences, though always by concrete and practical methods. True, at fifteen Emile 'has little knowledge, but what he has is really his; he knows nothing by halves'[184]. Moreover, he has 'only natural and purely physical knowledge'[185]. He has learned a manual trade. 'He knows the essential relations between man and things', but he does not know 'what metaphysics or morality are'. He can now be given a moral and religious training. This will culminate in the *Profession de Foi* of the touching Savoyard priest who helps him to find God in the spectacle of nature and in his own heart. Emile, now an accomplished young man, is finally introduced to the world. He soon meets Sophie, the natural girl, with whom he is of course destined to form a model couple.

It is difficult to imagine today how revolutionary such a programme seemed at a time when education was based largely on discipline and constraint, when children learned Latin at the tender age of six and when the emphasis was on training their memory rather than their judgment. But, if the pedagogical ideas in *Emile* are now part and parcel of our system and have therefore lost their freshness, the work itself is still as fresh as ever. The book is highly readable and full of surprises. Its infectious zest enlivens a wide variety of subjects, from cooking to theology. The reader is swept along on a floodtide of reflections, anecdotes and judgments. And all these have the rich tang of actual experience.

Nowadays one is tempted to think that *La Nouvelle Héloïse,* with all its interesting, delightful and touching passages, must have been above all a boring masterpiece. In fact it was tremendously successful, as Rousseau himself, though most dissatisfied with his contemporaries, was later to admit. Even before the book appeared, he recalled, 'the whole of Paris was dying to see this novel. The booksellers of the Rue Saint Jacques and of the Palais Royal were besieged by people demanding news of progress. When finally it came

The Vicar of Savoy leads Emile up a high hill
away from the town. 'Nature had spread out her
splendour before our eyes to provide us with
a subject for our discourse'. He then makes
to Emile his profession of belief in a God.
(Illustration by Marillier for book ɪv of *Emile*.)

out, its success was, most exceptionally, up to expectations'[186]. The novel, it will be remembered, is a long one and relates in the form of letters the moving story of (as the sub-title puts it) 'Two lovers in a small town at the foot of the Swiss Alps'. These are Julie d'Etange and her tutor Saint-Preux, a latter-day Abelard who has seduced her. This mutual love which is sanctioned by nature is condemned by society. Julie's father considers that Saint-Preux is of too humble birth to marry his daughter. In any case he has promised her to M. de Wolmar, to whom he is under an obligation. The marriage does in fact take place. Saint-Preux is in despair and contemplates committing suicide. Mme. de Wolmar, whom an inner voice in the depths of her heart has inspired with a feeling of respect for the sanctity of marriage, lives a life of virtue and tranquil happiness with her husband. Time goes by. Saint-Preux takes a trip round the world. Julie has children. M. de Wolmar knows about the past. He invites Julie's former lover, on his return, to come and live with them. Saint-Preux accepts. Soon after, M. de Wolmar goes away, leaving Saint-Preux alone with his wife. The two of them, despite temptations and inner struggles, emerge victorious from the trial. They are now cured. Saint-Preux has recovered his peace of mind, and takes over the education of Julie's children. Everything goes smoothly and merrily in the house. But Julie jumps into the lake to save one of the children, falls ill and dies, leaving everyone prostrate with grief.

What this simple but strange story sets out to prove is fairly clear. This is a veritable course in the teaching of virtue. Whereas novels are regarded as corrupting, this one should help to revive the moral sense, while profiting from the unhealthy vogue of the genre. 'Novels', observes Saint-Preux, 'are perhaps the last form of instruction which is still available for a people too corrupt for any other. I should therefore prefer the composition of this sort of book to be permitted only to decent but sensitive people whose heart was painted in their writings . . . who would not at once portray virtue as

*Je crois donc que le monde est gouverné
par une volonté puissante et sage.*

being in heaven and beyond the reach of man but which inspired
them with a love for it by painting it in less austere colours and then
found the way to lead them gently towards it from the bosom of
vice'[187]. It is thus that Julie, having had the revelation of her duties,
turns little by little and as it were effortlessly into a model wife. In
the same way Saint-Preux gradually fights his way out of despair.
In the end the two lovers, with M.de Wolmar, Mme. D'Orbe (Julie's
cousin) and Lord Edward (Saint-Preux's friend), form a natural
society founded on sincerity, respect of duty and the dignity of sentiment, a society purged of its prejudices and its taints. Since it is not
possible to revert to a state of nature, the essential point is to re-
introduce in society, as far as possible, those virtues which nature
teaches. In Paris, Saint-Preux remarks, 'it seems as if the whole order
of natural feelings is inverted. The heart does not lead to a bond.
Girls are not permitted to have a heart. This right is reserved for
married women, and extends to all apart from their husbands. It is
better for a mother to have a score of lovers than for her daughter to
have one. Nobody is revolted at adultery'[188]. *Héloïse,* both when
it deals with Julie as a girl and as a wife, marks here as elsewhere a
striking return to what Rousseau regards as the natural order.

Admittedly, once it is restored this order cannot be guaranteed
to last unless mankind reverts to the initial pact which constitutes
society. For it is the *Contrat Social* which safeguards the rights of the
individual while establishing a legitimate government. In the book
bearing this title, which forms the heart of Rousseau's political work,
he defines the contract with the stringency, the clarity and even the
dryness of a rigid theorist. But we have to go to *Héloïse* for the
concrete picture, with its rich spectrum, of the constitution of a
small society living according to nature. It presupposes a reformation in every walk of life. And hence the reader is offered disquisitions on a host of topics – Italian and French music, duels, the
aristocracy, the opera, suicide, domestic economy, education,

luxury, the construction of gardens, how to administer property and so on. In fact the principles underlying this wide range of judgments are always the same. We must return to simple tastes, manners and feelings. Life in the country gives man the only happiness made for him, that of feeling at one with nature. Even as early as 1758 in his *Letter to D'Alembert*, while stressing the basic immorality of the theatre and especially of Molière's plays, and condemning the shows which constitute the main diversion in towns, Rousseau extols the innocent pleasures of rustic life and clean living. Here he illustrates with a greater wealth of detail the theme which he had touched on then. But of course this whole conversion is effected within and through sentiment. This is what creates the unity of action and doctrine in the novel.

Héloïse is above all a slowly unfolding poem of love and sacrifice into which Jean-Jacques has poured his ideas, his fervent enthusiasm and his raptures. This laying bare of a heart was a novel experience at the time, and fascinated readers. Love, nature and virtue are merged and almost reduced to one in the same poetic sweep. Passion no longer stops short at the heart. It gives life to the landscape and picturesqueness to the mountains. As for the feeling for nature, the privilege of men and women of feeling, it is itself linked to a moral and religious effusion, to a fundamental goodness and to inner purity. 'Atheists', said Rousseau, 'do not like the country'[189]. Here is the source of the close relation which seemed normal from 1770 on, but which may appear strange nowadays, between botany and morality. Bernardin de Saint-Pierre was later to combine, without causing anyone to bat an eyelid, the functions of Director of the Botanical Garden and Professor of Moral Philosophy at the Ecole Normale Supérieure. This seems to be the conclusion of this huge movement to re-integrate man with his own nature and with nature in general. The edifice now seems complete, with the peristyle of the two *Discourses* and the *Letter to D'Alembert* and with the three massive blocks of the *Héloïse,* the *Contrat* and *Emile.* As it is, Jean-Jacques, at grips with the real or imaginary persecutions which followed the condemnation of *Emile* in Paris and Geneva, turns aside from his writing and even occasionally regrets his past efforts.

However, far from giving up writing, he now completes his plan by enabling the reader to penetrate into the very heart of natural man, for whose restoration he had laboured so well. And natural man is no other than himself. True, as we have seen, he had always been present in his books, and he was still so deeply embedded in them that what the reader finds there is always Rousseau himself. But from now on he becomes the only subject of his work, and we pass from the philosopical treatise to real life, from an ideology to its incarnation, from the novel of imagined events to that of actual experience or recollection. Admittedly he no longer addresses the same public. Neither the *Confessions,* written in 1765–7 and in 1769–70, nor the *Rêveries* composed in his last two years (1776–8), were published during his lifetime. Disappointed in his contemporaries, it is among his readers of the future that he seeks the brothers and devotees whom he had always needed. But this audience puts him all the more at his ease. He feels he can tell it everything; he can dig down to the bedrock of nature and make them discover in him, as though in a living organism, the truths which Julie, Saint-Preux and Emile had already suggested to them.

In the opening lines of the *Confessions* he writes: 'I am about to engage in an undertaking of which there is no previous example and which will not, once executed, be copied. I wish to show my fellow-beings a man in his whole natural sincerity, and this man will be I myself. I alone.' In fact this venture was to have a host of imitators. It marks the start of a whole literature of exhibitionism. But above all, far from being the effect of an unexpected and bizarre decision, it is the normal and almost inevitable consequence of the author's previous steps. When he was dealing with education, he had had to imagine a child of nature called Emile. But there is no need to invent natural man when recounting his tribulations in a corrupt society. That man exists and he is Jean-Jacques. The *Confessions*, then, especially in their first part which stops in 1740 when Rousseau was twenty-eight, conjure up the unique adventure of a man who is different from all other men. 'I dare to believe', he writes, 'that I am not like any other existing creature'.

Now what happens is that everyone of us, when he goes back to his original innocence and feels redeemed by the generous urges of his heart, enters this man's world and becomes identified with him. The power of youth and purity is infectious. The reader accompanies Jean-Jacques in his quest for the past and goes back with him to his verdant paradise. Like the child poet of Baudelaire and by the same means, 'in all he sees and all he touches', the author of the *Confessions* 'finds ambrosia and rosy nectar'. There are some marvellous pages in this book; indeed they are among the most felicitous in French literature. In this luminous past created by the poet, the vigorous and unfettered happiness of natural man bursts forth with triumphant freshness. The power of such magic to conquer the reader is certainly even greater than that of the *Discourses* or *Héloïse*. But the direction is the same.

One of the secrets of this youthfulness and moral innocence is the complete and perpetual coincidence between man and what he feels, that is, sincerity. The man who obeys the law of nature is devoid of disingenuousness or mental reservations. He hides nothing and is completely open. If he sometimes errs, at least he does so without malice, and, by immediately confessing what he has done, he proves the purity of his intentions and in a way effaces his errors. Under the seal of secrecy, Rousseau confided to his friends that he had once abandoned to public charity, one after the other, all of his five children. His friends revealed the secret. There is no common denominator between his fault and theirs. Jean-Jacques allowed himself to be led astray by ideas which he later regarded as wrong. 'My fault is great', he admits, 'but it was a mistake. I neglected my duties, but no desire to do harm entered my heart, and the bowels of a father can never be deeply stirred by children whom he has never set eyes on. But to betray the trust of friendship, to violate the most holy of pledges, to broadcast secrets poured into one's ear, to wantonly dishonour the friend whom one has betrayed . . . these are not offences, they are contemptible and sordid acts'[190]. The intention really shapes the act. The material results have a certain importance but they cannot confer a moral colouring or a particular gravity on the action which led to them.

Thirty years after Rousseau's death, a writer expressed astonishment at the effects of this doctrine stressing the crucial importance of intentions and of sincerity which lies at the very heart of the *Confessions*. 'It is certainly very singular', he wrote, 'to witness a man who seeks to obtain the esteem and even the admiration of posterity by communicating the slightest details of a life which has nothing great about it . . . and which on the contrary is filled with ignoble details and unpardonable turpitudes. But there is something even more surprising, and that is the success of such an enterprise. He managed to persuade people how virtuous he was, while he most palpably was not. This proves what a powerful effect the painting of a vivid and convincing impression makes on the heart of man, what a favourable response it arouses'[191]. *The painting of a vivid and convincing impression* – in fact the success of the *Confessions* flows above all from their tone, the rhythm of the phrase, in their style, halfway between Voltaire and Chateaubriand, which gives words a weight of their own, a colour, without detracting from the intellectual preciseness, an invisible and enchanting style which is admirably suited to the triple poetry of sentiment, youth and recollection. For this and for many other reasons, the *Rêveries* appear to be the continuation and culmination of the *Confessions*.

These walks in the surroundings of Paris are poetic reveries of mind and heart which have something of the philosophical meditation about them, of the *étude* in the musical sense of the word. 'Sometimes my reveries ended in meditation, but more often my meditations finished in a reverie, and, during these exaltations, my soul hovers over the universe on the wings of fantasy in ecstasies which surpass all other delights'[192]. Jean-Jacques, with a completely sober simplicity, goes straight to the soul, carries his quest to the end to find the unmediated and the fundamental in man; when everything has abandoned him, he still retains the plenitude of simply existing. 'As soon as I let myself unbend', he writes, 'again I become what nature intended. This, whatever is done to destroy it, is my most constant state, and the one by virtue of which, in spite of fate, I enjoy a happiness for which I feel I am made'[193]. Cut off from his fellowmen by the persecution mania which had haunted him for fifteen years, 'alone on earth', as he say himself, 'having neither brother, neighbour nor friend[194]', Jean-Jacques never touched the hearts of his readers more deeply or won their fraternal sympathy more fully. Even today, Frenchmen who do not know Voltaire's first name and who would never dream of referring to Diderot as 'Denis' or to Valéry as 'Paul' call Rousseau 'Jean-Jacques' in a sort of affectionate familiarity, as if he were closer to them, more at home with them than any other of their great writers.

Thus Rousseau can switch from an academic discourse to a novel, from a dogmatic treatise to an autobiography, from philosophy to lyricism. In his vast and astonishingly varied work we find the extraordinary continuity of a grand design. There is an approach which is typical of Montesquieu, a wit that is Voltaire's alone, a genius peculiar to Diderot, but there is a universe of Jean-Jacques which has become our own. For Rousseau is one of the real founders of the modern world, but we are not conscious of the fact any more than we are of the air we breathe. The literature of the individual, personal lyricism, the glorification of feeling, poetic prose, collectivism as well as democracy, the active method in modern pedagogy, hydrotherapy, psychoanalysis, mountaineering, the cult of the genuine, all these and a hundred other aspects of our civilisation would never exist, or at least not in their present form, if Rousseau had not written his works. If today there is some reluctance in French schools to tell children their marks in public, this is perhaps because of a passage in the *Discourse on Inequality* in which Rousseau studies the question of success in competitions for singing, dancing and eloquence among the men of primitive times, noting 'From these first preferences were born on the one hand vanity and contempt, and on the other shame and envy'[195]. In 1745 the Abbé Prévost, at the beginning of his *Mémoires d'un honnête homme,* shows the reader his unfortunate hero. He is a prisoner at Innsbruck in a room 'from which the only view was of a wild chain of mountains'[196]. If tourists today would fight for such a room, this is in part because Rousseau has helped to invent nature, and indeed the very institution of holidays in the country or winter sports owes much to him. In a word, whether one loves Rousseau or whether one deplores his influence, to read his work is first of all to give oneself up to the charm of a keen analysis and of a seductive diction. It is also, for anyone living in our present civilisation, to accomplish a pilgrimage back to its sources.

1 **General Bibliography for the seventeenth and eighteenth centuries**
A.Coiranescu, *Bibliographie de la littérature française du* XVIIe *siècle,*
C.N.R.S., 3 vols, 1966. D.C.Cabeen and J.Brody, *A Critical Bibliography
of French Literature,* Syracuse University Press; vol. III, *The Seventeenth
Century,* 1961; vol. IV, *The Eighteenth Century,* 1951. R.L.Graeme Ritchie
(ed.), *France: A Companions to French Studies,* 4th ed., Methuen, 1946.
W.A.Nitze and E.P.Dargan, *A History of French Literature,* Holt,
Rinehart and Winston, 3rd ed., 1965. A.L.Guérard, *The Life and Death
of an Ideal: France in the Classical Age,* Scribner, 1928, repr., Allen, 1957.
W.G.Moore, *French Classical Literature,* Oxford University Press, 1961.
J.-J.Demorest (ed.), *Studies in Seventeenth-Century French Literature,*
Cornell University Press, 1962. J.Cruickshank (ed.), *French Literature
and Its Background,* vol. III, *The Eighteenth Century,* Oxford University
Press, 1968. G.Saintsbury, *A History of the French Novel,* vol. I,
Macmillan (London), 1917. P.A.Chapman (ed.), *Anthology of Eight-
eenth-Century French Literature,* Princeton University Press, 1930.

2 **The religious, philosophical or analytical literature of the seventeenth
century**
The Philosophical Works of Descartes, 2 vols., E.S.Haldane and
G.R.T.Ross, Dover, 1955. *Essential Works of Descartes,* tr. L.Bair,
intro. by D.J.Bronstein, Bantam, 1961. *Bossuet. A Prose Anthology,*
ed. J.Standring, Harrap, 1962. La Rochefoucauld, *Maxims,* tr. and
intro. by L.W.Tancock, Penguin, 1959. *The Maxims of Rochefoucauld,*
tr. L.Kronenberger, Random House, 1959. *Letters from Madame la
Marquise de Sévigné,* tr. and intro. by V.Hammersley, Secker and
Warburg, 1955.

   N.Abercrombie, *The Origins of Jansenism,* Clarendon Press, 1936.
A.G.A.Balz, *Descartes and the Modern Mind,* Yale University Press,
1952. W.Doney (ed.), *Descartes: A Collection of Critical Essays,*
Macmillan, 1968. A.Tilley, *Madame de Sévigné: Some Aspects of Her
Life and Character,* Cambridge, 1936.

3 **Pascal**
Oeuvres complètes, ed. Brunschvicg and Boutroux, Grands Ecrivains de
la France, 1904–8, Hachette, 12 vols. *Pensées,* small edn. Brunschvicg,

Hachette. The numbers after the quotations refer to this edn. *Pensées,* ed. Lafuma, Delmas, 1952. *Great Shorter Works,* tr. and intro. by E. Cailliet and J. C. Blankenagel, Westminster Press (Philadelphia), 1948. (Includes major works except for *Pensées* and *Provinciales*). *The Essential Pascal,* tr. G. F. Pullen, ed. and intro. by R. W. Gleason, S. J., New English Library, New American Library, 1966. *Pensées,* bilingual French/English edn.; tr. and intro. by H. F. Stewart, Routledge and Kegan Paul, Pantheon, 1950. *Pensées,* Brunschvicg edn.; tr. W. F. Trotter, intro. by T. S. Eliot, Dent, E. P. Dutton, 1954. *Pensées,* Lafuma ed.; tr. and intro. by M. Turnell, Harvill Press, 1962. *The Provincial Letters,* tr. and intro. by A. J. Krailsheimer, Penguin, 1967.

J. Mesnard, *Pascal: His Life and Works,* Philosophical Library (New York), 1952. H. Peyre, 'Friends and Foes of Pascal in France Today', *Yale French Studies,* Fall-Winter, 1953. E. Mortimer, *Blaise Pascal, the Life and Work of a Realist,* Methuen, 1959. E. Cailliet, *Pascal: The Emergence of Genius,* 2nd edn., Harper Brothers, 1961. J. Steinmann, *Pascal,* Harcourt, Brace and World, 1966.

4 *Variation sur une Pensée, Variété I,* The following quotation is taken from this study.

5 *Memorial* found in Pascal's coat after his death. Small Brunschvicg edn., p. 142.

6 *Mélanges,* p. 104, (see notes 94 and 110).

7 *Les caractères,* ed. G. Cayrou, Didier, 1950. *Characters,* tr. H. van Laun, intro. by D. C. Potts, Oxford University Press, 1963.

8 Preface to the *Caractères* (addition first published in 1690).

9 'The new *Caractères,* by first unfolding the thoughts, feelings and impulses of men, uncover the principle underlying their malice and their weaknesses, and thus enable the reader to have no difficulty in anticipating everything which they are capable of saying and doing, and preventing him from being any longer surprised at innumerable vicious and frivolous actions with which their life is filled.' *Discours sur Théophraste.*

10 Corbinelli, *Sentiments d'Amour tirés des meilleurs poètes,* Barbin, Paris, 1685, 2 vols., notice prefixed to vol. I.

11 In vol. I (1654) of *Clélie,* Mlle de Scudéry's novel.

12 Preface to 1688 edition (at the end).

13 *Discours sur Théophraste* (towards the end).

14 Speech on his reception by the French Academy (1927). Reproduced in *Variété IV,* Bibliothèque de la Pléiade, vol. I, p. 7.

15 **Seventeenth-century poetry**
R. Picard, *La poésie française de 1640 à 1680.* S.E.D.E.S., 1964–9, 2 vols. G. Brereton (ed.), *The Penguin Book of French Verse,* vol. II: *The*

Sixteenth to the Eighteenth Century, 1958. O.de Mourgues, *Metaphysical, Baroque and Précieux Poetry*, Oxford University Press, 1953. R.Winegarten, *French Lyric Poetry in the Age of Malherbe*, Manchester University Press, 1954.

16 Primi Visconti, *Mémoires*, ed. Lemoine, Hachette, 1908, pp. 226.

17 **Malherbe**
Malherbe, *Oeuvres*, ed. Lalanne, Grands Ecrivains de la France 1862–9, 5 vols., Hachette.
    A.M.Boase, 'Then Malherbe Came', *Criterion*, vol. 10, 1930–1. E.W.Gosse. *Malherbe and the Classical Reactions in the Seventeenth Century*, Clarendon Press, 1920.

18 *Art Poétique* (1674), canto I, l. 131.
19 Racan, *Vie de Malherbe, ed. cit.* (Lalanne), vol. I, pp. LXXVI and LXXVII.
20 Tallemant des Réaux, *Historiettes*, ed. Adam, Bibliothèque de la Pléiade, vol. I, p. 108, quoting Balzac.
21 Racan, *op. cit.*, p. LXXX. This passage refers to translations by Malherbe but the remark seems applicable to his poetry as well.
22 *Sonnet* for Mme d'Auchy (1608).
23 *L'oeuvre et la vie de Delacroix, Oeuvres complètes*, ed. Le Dantec, Bibliothèque de la Pléiade, 1961, p. 1126.
24 *Ode à la Reine Mère sur les heureux succès de sa Régence*, 1610 (at the end).
25 Tallemant, *loc. cit.*
26 *Variété V*, p. 171.
27 *Paraphrase du Psaume CXXVIII.*
28 *Fragment* (1625).
29 Published in 1600.

30 **La Fontaine**
Oeuvres complètes, ed. H.Régnier, Grands Ecrivains de la France, 1833–93, Hachette, 11 vols. *Oeuvres diverses* (all except *Fables* and *Contes*). ed. P.Clarac, Bibliothèque de la Pléiade, Gallimard, 1958. *Selected Works of La Fontaine*, ed. P.A.Wadsworth, Harper Brothers, 1950. *La Fontaine's Fables*, verse tr. Sir Edward Marsh, Dent, E.P.Dutton, 1952. *The Complete Fables*, verse tr. with original rhyme scheme R.Jarman, New English Library, 1962.
P.A.Wadsworth, *Young La Fontaine*, Evanston (Illinois), 1952. M. Sutherland, *La Fontaine*, Cape, 1953. M.Guiton, *La Fontaine, Poet and*

239

Counterpoet, Rutgers University Press, 1961. J.D.Biard, *The Style of La Fontaine's Fables*, Basil Blackwell, 1966.

31 Dédicace au Dauphin (1668).

32 Epître à Monseigneur l'evêque de Soissons [Huet] (1687). *Oeuvres diverses, ed. cit.*, p. 648.

33 Chamfort, *Eloge de La Fontaine* (1774). *Oeuvres choisies de La Fontaine*, Cazin, 1782, pp. 17-18.

34 Review by Charles Perrault in *Les hommes illustres qui ont paru en France* (1696).

35 Corrected version of an *Eloge de La Fontaine*, text for translation into Latin set for the Duke of Bourgogne by Fénelon (tr.), *Oeuvres complètes, ed. cit.*, vol. I, p. CCXI.

36 Corneille, Analysis of *Andromède* (1660).

37 **The theatre in the seventeenth century**
Apart from Corneille, Molière and Racine, see the editions of Théophile de Viau (*Pyrame et Thisbé*), Hardy, Mairet, Tristan, Rotrou, Thomas Corneille, in *Les contemporains de Molière* (ed. V.Fournel, Didot, 1863–75, 3 vols.) etc.

H.C.Lancaster, *A History of French Dramatic Literature in the Seventeenth Century*, 9 vols., Johns Hopkins Press, 1929–42. R.Lowenstein, *Voltaire as an Historian of Seventeenth-Century French Drama*, Johns Hopkins Press, 1935. M.Turnell, *The Classical Moment: Studies Of Corneille, Molière and Racine*, New Directions, 1948. L.Lockert, *The Chief Rivals of Corneille and Racine*, Vanderbilt University Press (Nashville), 1956. D.Roaten, *Structural Forms in the French Theater, 1500–1700*, Philadelphia, 1960. D.A.Collins, *Thomas Corneille: Protean Dramatist*, Mouton and Co. (The Hague), 1966. C.Cherpack, *The Call of Blood in French Classical Tragedy*, Johns Hopkins Press, 1958.

38 **Corneille**
Oeuvres complètes, ed. Marty-Laveaux, Grands Ecrivains de la France, 1862–8, Hachette, 12 vols. L.Lockert, *The Chief Plays of Corneille*, blank verse tr., Princeton University Press, 1952. L.Lockert, *More Plays of Corneille*, blank verse tr., Vanderbilt University Press, 1959. S.Solomon, *Pierre Corneille, Seven Plays*, Random House, 1969.

D.F.Canfield, *Corneille and Racine in England*, Columbia University Press, 1904. L.M.Riddle, *The Genesis and Sources of Pierre Corneille's Tragedies from Médée to Pertharite*, Johns Hopkins Studies in Romance Literature and Language, vol. 3, 1926. P.J.Yarrow, *Corneille*, Macmillan, 1963. R.J.Nelson, *Corneille: His Heroes and Their Worlds*,

University of Pennsylvania Press, 1963.

39 *Excusatio*, l. 21–4, (tr.), ed. Le Seuil, p. 869.

40 **Molière**

Oeuvres complètes, ed. Despois-Mesnard, Grands Ecrivains de la France, 1873–1900, Hachette, 13 vols. *Molière's Comedies*, 2 vols., tr. H.Baker and J.Miller, Dent, E.P.Dutton, 1956. *Six Prose Comedies of Molière*, tr. G.Graveley, Oxford University Press, 1956. *The Misanthrope and Other Plays*, tr. J.Wood, Penguin, 1959.

W.G.Moore, *Molière, a New Criticism*, Oxford University Press, 1949. J.D.Hubert, *Molière and the Comedy of Intellect*, University of California Press, 1962. L.Gossman, *Men and Masks: A Study of Molière*, Johns Hopkins Press, 1965.

41 *Lettre sur 'l'imposteur'*, *Oeuvres complètes*, ed. Despois-Mesnard, vol. IV, p. 555.

42 **Racine**

Oeuvres complètes, ed. P.Mesnard, Grands Ecrivains de la France, 1885–8, Hachette, 8 vols. *Oeuvres complètes*, ed. R.Picard, Bibliothèque de la Pléiade, 1966–8, 2 vols. *Racine's Mid-Career Tragedies*, rhyming verse tr. L.Lockert, Princeton University Press, 1958. *Five Plays*, verse tr. K.Muir, MacGibbon and Kee, 1960. *Andromache and Other Plays*. *Phaedra and Other Plays*, tr. John Cairncross, 2 vols., Penguin, 1963–8. *The Best Plays of Racine*, rhyming verse tr. L.Lockert, Princeton University Press, 1966. *The Complete Plays of Jean Racine*, tr. S.Solomon, 2 vols., Random House, 1967, Weidenfeld and Nicolson, 1969.

K.E.Wheatley, *Racine and English Classicism*, University of Texas Press, 1956. R.C.Knight, 'On Translating Racine', *Studies in Modern French Literature*, Manchester University Press, 1961. L.Goldmann, *The Hidden God: A Study of Tragic Vision in the 'Pensées' of Pascal and the Tragedies of Racine*, Routledge and Kegan Paul, The Humanities Press (N.Y.), 1964. P.France, *Racine's Rhetoric*, Clarendon Press, 1965. O.de Mourgues, *Racine or the Triumph of Relevance*, Cambridge University Press, 1967.

43 *Polyeucte*, II, 2.

44 **The seventeenth-century novel**

Romanciers du XVIIe siècle, (*Francion*, *Roman comique*, *Roman bourgeois*), ed. A.Adam, Bibliothèque de la Pléiade, 1962. Mme de la Fayette, *The Princess of Clèves*, tr. N.Mitford, Penguin, 1961; tr. W.J.Cobb, New American Library of World Literature, 1961. Mme de la Fayette,

241

La Princesse de Montpensier, and *La Comtesse de Tende,* Saint-Réal, *La conjuration des Espagnols* and *Don Carlos* and other texts are to be published shortly, ed. R.Picard in *Nouvelles des XVII*e *et XVIII*e *siècles,* Bibliothèque de la Pléiade. D.McDougall, *Madeleine de Scudéry,* Methuen, 1938.

45 This is the pejorative expression used by Nicole to designate Desmarets. See R.Picard, *Racine polémiste,* Pauvert, 1967, p. 22.

46 Huet, *Traité de l'origine des romans,* published in the same volume as *Zaïde,* a novel by Mme de La Fayette, in 1670, (at the beginning).

47 Desmarets de Saint Sorlin, Preface to *Ariane* (1639 edn.).

48 Du Plaisir, *Sentiment sur les romans* (1683).

49 *La Bibliothèque Française,* ch. IX.

50 In addition to the A. Adam edn. (see note 44), see edn. E. Magne, Geneva, Droz, 1950 to which the page numbers following the quotations refer.

51 (Valincourt), *Lettres à la Marquise *** sur la Princesse de Clèves* (1678). Bossard, 1922, p. 111.

52 *Mercure Galant,* special number July 1678, pp. 215-6.

53 Valincourt, p. 190.

54 Letter to Lescheraine (1678), ed. Magne, p. XXXII.

55 **The eighteenth-century theatre**
I.O.Wade, *The 'Philosophe' in the French Drama of the Eighteenth Century,* Princeton, 1926. H.C.Lancaster, *French Tragedy in the Time of Louis XV and Voltaire,* Johns Hopkins Press, 1950.

56 Prologue of *Le Port à l'Anglais ou les nouvelles débarquées,* comedy by Autreau, *Oeuvres,* Briasson, 1749, vol. I, p. 7.

57 *Troisième entretien sur le Fils naturel. Oeuvres complètes,* ed. Assézat, vol. VII, pp. 134, 150-1.

58 The *Proverbes* appeared from 1768 to 1781 (in 8 vols.).

59 **Marivaux**
Théâtre complet, ed. F.Deloffre, Garnier 1968, 2 vols.
A.Tilley, 'Marivaux', *Three French Dramatists,* Cambridge University Press, 1933. K.McKee, *The Theatre of Marivaux,* Peter Owen, 1959.

60 Very interesting review by D'Alembert, reproduced in the Le Seuill edn.,

61 Formula of Marivaux's, *Spectateur Français* (1723), quoted by F. Deloffre, p. 148 (edn. Belles-Lettres).

62 The first *Surprise de l'Amour* was created by the Italian Comedians in 1722. The second, intended for the French Comedians, was performed in 1727.

63 D'Alembert, *loc. cit.*

64 Preface to the edition of Marivaux's *Oeuvres Diverses,* Duchesne, 1765, vol. I, p. X.

65 *Foreword* of the *Serments Indiscrets.*

66 Quoted by D'Alembert, *loc. cit.*

67 The words in italics attributed to Marivaux by D'Alembert are commented on by him, *loc. cit.*

68 **Beaumarchais**
   Oeuvres complètes, ed. Moland, Garnier, 1874. *Théâtre complet,* ed. Allem and Paul-Courant, Bibliothèque de la Pléiade, 1957. *The Barber of Seville,* and *The Marriage of Figaro,* tr. J. Wood, Penguin, 1964.
   J.B.Ratermanis and W.R.Irwin, *The Comic Style of Beaumarchais,* University of Washington Press, 1961. C.Cox, *The Real Figaro,* Longmans, 1962.

69 Preface to the *Barbier de Séville,* edn. de la Pléiade, p. 157.

70 Preface to the *Mariage de Figaro, ibid.,* p. 240.

71 *Ibid.,* p. 237.

72 *Ibid.,* p. 236.

73 **The eighteenth-century novel**
   For Prévost, Marivaux and Laclos, see below. Novels by Le Sage, Crébillon, Duclos, Louvet de Couvray, Sénac de Meilhan, etc. will be found in *Romanciers du XVIIIe siècle,* ed. Etiemble, Bibliothèque de la Pléiade, 2 vols., *Les Illustres Françaises* by Challes are ed. by F.Deloffre in the *Nouvelles françaises des XVIIe et XVIIIe siècles,* Bibliothèque de la Pléiade. J.G.Palache, *Four Novelists of the Old Régime* (Crébillon, Laclos, Diderot, Restif de la Bretonne), Viking Press (N.Y.), 1926. F.C.Green, *French Novelists: Manners and Ideas from the Renaissance to the Revolution,* New York, 1929. C.Cherpack, *An Essay on Crébillon Fils,* Duke University Press, 1962. V.Mylne, *The Eighteenth-Century French Novel,* Manchester University Press, 1965.

74 By the Abbé de la Porte, Paris, 1777, IV, (at the beginning and p. 102).

75 Letter to Thieriot of 28 December 1735, *Correspondence,* ed. Besterman, vol. I, p. 628.

76 **The Abbé Prévost**
   Oeuvres choisies, Hotel Serpente, 1783 *et seq.,* or Leblanc, 1810 *et seq.,* 39 vols. *Manon Lescaut,* ed. F.Deloffre and R.Picard, Garnier, 1965.

The numbers after the quotations refer to this edition. *Manon Lescaut,* tr. L.W.Tancock, Penguin, 1949.

G.R.Harvers, *The Abbé Prévost and English Literature,* Princeton University Press, 1921. H.Kurz, *Manon Lescaut: A Study in Unchanging Critics,* Columbia University Press, 1930.

77 *Oeuvres choisies* 1810, vol. XI, p. 8.

78 *Ibid.,* vol. I, (Preface), p. 56.

79 Marivaux, novelist

La vie de Marianne, ed. F.Deloffre, Garnier, 1957. *Le paysan parvenu,* ed. F.Deloffre, Garnier, 1959. *Oeuvres diverses,* ed. F.Deloffre, Garnier, 1969. The references after the quotations refer to these editions.

F.Deloffre, *Marivaux et le marivaudage,* Colin, 1968. R.K.Jamieson, *Marivaux: A Study in Eighteenth Century Sensibility,* King's Crown Press (N.Y.), 1941.

80 Montjoie, *Histoire de la conjuration de L: P.J.d'Orléans.* Paris, chez les marchands de nouveautés, 1800, vol. V, p. 30.

Laclos

Oeuvres complètes, ed. Allem, Bibliothèque de la Pléiade, 1951. *Dangerous Acquaintances,* tr. R.Aldington, New English Library, 1962. *Dangerous Liaisons,* tr. L.Bair, intro. by André Maurois, Bantam, 1962.

D.Thelander, *Laclos and the Epistolary Novel,* Librairie Droz (Geneva), 1963.

81 Tilly, *Mémoires* (1828), quoted by Allem, p. 710.

Literature and philosophy in the eighteenth century

82 *Caractères,* I, 65. Text already commented on above on p. 30.

G.Boas, *The Happy Beast in French Thought of the Eighteenth Century,* Johns Hopkins Press, 1933. C.Becker, *The Heavenly City of the Eighteenth-Century Philosophers,* Yale University Press, 1952. E.Beller and M.du P.Lee, Jr., *Selections from Bayle's Dictionary,* Princeton University Press, 1952. F.E.Manuel, *The Eighteenth Century Confronts the Gods,* Harvard University Press, 1959. L.G.Crocker, *An Age of Crisis: Man and World in Eighteenth-Century French Thought,* Johns Hopkins Press, 1959.

83 Diderot, *La promenade du sceptique,* (1747), *Oeuvres complètes,* ed. Assézat et Tourneux, vol. I, p. 184.

84 Letter to Voltaire (of 29 September 1762), *Correspondance,* ed. Roth, vol. IV, p. 176–7.

85 *Correspondence,* ed. Besterman, vol. LII, pp. 265-6 (Appendix 149).

86 Article on *Encyclopédie,* Diderot, *Oeuvres complètes,* ed. Assézat, vol. XIV, p. 415.

87 Article on *Vomit.* 'This is also said in the figurative sense: *to vomit abuse'.* Diderot had suggested as an example, 'The abuse which the Fathers of the Church vomited against each other'. Gordon Torrey, *The censorship of Diderot's Encyclopédie,* Columbia University Press, 1947, p. 107.

88 Letter to Sophie Volland (of 3 October 1762). *Correspondance,* ed. Roth, vol. IV, p. 186.

89 **Montesquieu**

Lettres Persanes, ed. A.Adam, Geneva, Droz, 1954. *Oeuvres complètes,* ed. R.Caillois. Bibliothèque de la Pléiade, Gallimard, 1949–51, 2 vols. *Persian Letters,* tr. J.Davidson, Broadway Translations (London), 1923.

P.M.Spurlin, *Montesquieu in America, 1760–1801,* Louisiana, State University Press, 1940. G.Saintsbury, 'Montesquieu', *French Literature and its Masters,* Knopf, 1946. R.Shackleton, *Montesquieu: A Critical Biography,* Oxford University Press, 1961.

90 *Mes Pensées. Oeuvres complètes, ed. cit.,* vol. I, p. 975.

91 P.Valéry, *La soirée avec M.Teste* (remark attributed to M.Teste).

92 *Mes Pensées, ed. cit.,* vol. I, p. 978.

93 *Voyages, ed. cit.,* vol. I, p. 879.

94 **Voltaire**

Oeuvres complètes, ed. Moland (text by Beuchot for works previously published). Garnier, 1877–82, 52 vols., referred to hereafter as *Moland.* Voltaire's *Correspondence,* ed. T.Besterman, Geneva. Institut Voltaire, 1953–67, 107 vols. An abbreviated edition has been published by the Bibliothèque de la Pléiade. *Mélanges,* ed. Van den Heuvel, Gallimard, Bibliothèque de la Pléiade, 1961; referred to as *Mélanges. Oeuvres historiques,* ed. R.Pomeau, Bibliothèque de la Pléiade, 1957; referred to as *Oeuvres historiques. Selected Works of Voltaire,* tr. J.McCabe, Watts and Co. (London), 1948. R.L.Graeme Ritchie, *Voltaire: A Prose Anthology,* Nelson, 1927. *The Living Thoughts of Voltaire,* presented by André Maurois, Longmans (N.Y.), 1939. *Candide, and Other Tales,* Smollet's tr., revised J.Thornton, Dent, E.P.Dutton, 1955. *Voltaire's Philosophical Dictionary,* selected and tr. H.I.Woolf, Allen and Unwin. 1945. *Voltaire's Micromégas,* (A study in the fusion of science, myth and art), ed. intro. and notes I.O.Wade, Princeton University Press.

1950. *Select Letters of Voltaire,* tr. and ed. T.Besterman, Nelson, 1963. *The Philosophy of History,* preface T.Kiernan (repr. of original edn. of 1766), Vision (London), 1965.

N.L.Torrey, *The Spirit of Voltaire,* Columbia University Press, 1938. G.Lanson, *Voltaire,* John Wiley and Sons (N.Y.), 1960. H.T.Mason, *Pierre Bayle and Voltaire,* Oxford University Press, 1963. R.H.Gross, *Voltaire: Nonconformist,* Vision, 1968.

95 It is very rare for Voltaire to be guilty of complete nonsense, as when, lagging behind the geology of his age and unwilling to grasp the significance of fossils, he suggested that the shells found on the Mont Cenis might well have fallen from the bonnets of pilgrims to Saint James of Compostella. *Des singularités de la nature,* ch. xii, (1768), Moland, vol. 27, pp. 145–6.

96 Brunschvicg 139. Voltaire did not have access to the exact text which reads, 'when we think carefully about it'.

97 *Mélanges,* pp. 112–9.

98 *Ibid.,* p. 110. Voltaire often laughed at the idle speculations of traditional philosophy. 'The inventors of mechanical arts' he wrote at the end of the article on *Philosophy* in his *Philosophical Dictionary,* 'have been much more useful to mankind than the inventors of syllogisms: the man who invented the weaver's shuttle is infinitely better than the man who conceived of innate ideas'.

99 *Ibid.,* p. 121.

100 *Avis au public sur les parricides imputés aux Calas et aux Sirven* (1766), *Mélanges,* p. 835.

101 *Examen de Milord Bolingbroke, Mélanges,* p. 1047.

102 *Mélanges,* p. 270.

103 Ed. Fabre, 1963, p. 42.

104 *Mélanges,* pp. 638–9.

105 *Moland,* vol. 21, p. 556.

106 Article on *Providence* in *Questions sur l'Encyclopédie* (1771). *Mélanges,* p. 1307.

107 Voltaire cannot help giving way to fatalism when he considers certain historical concatenations. Having outlined the life of Lolly Tollendal, he writes in his *Précis du Siècle de Louis XV,* 'If anything is capable of persuading us that it is fate which governs the chaotic events making up the politics of the world, it is the sight of an Irishman driven from his country with his king's family, commanding French troops six thousand leagues away in a traders' war on shores unknown to Alexander, Genghis Khan and Tamerlane, executed on the banks of the Seine for having

been captured by the English in the ancient Gulf of the Ganges.' *Oeuvres historiques*, p. 1506.

108 *Candide*, ch. xx, *Moland*, vol. 21, p. 184.

109 *Ibid.*, ch. xxx, p. 215.

110 *Lettres philosophiques*, 25th letter, *Mélanges*, p. 104.

111 *Ibid.*, p. 110.

112 *Le Mondain* (1736), lines 9–10. *Mélanges*, p. 932.

113 *Ibid.*, p. 206, (last line).

114 *André Destouches à Siam*, *Mélanges*, p. 932.

115 *Ibid.*, p. 933.

116 Ch. i, Intro., *Oeuvres historiques*, p. 616.

117 *Nouvelles considérations sur l'histoire* (1744), *Oeuvres historiques*, p. 47.

118 *Le pyrrhonisme et l'histoire* (1768), ch. xvi. *Moland*, vol. 27, p. 266.

119 *Epîtres aux fidèles par le grand apôtre des Délices* (1763), *Correspondence*, ed. Besterman, vol. lii, p. 265, appendice 149.

120 *Mélanges*, p. 312.

121 *Ibid.*, p. 681.

122 *Ibid.*, p. 712.

123 *Rolla*, iv (1833).

124 *Soirées de Saint-Petersbourg, Quatrième Entretien*, Librairie grecque, latine et française, 1821. He also sees on Voltaire's face 'the lips pinched by a cruel malice like a spring ready to uncoil and launch torrents of blasphemy and sarcasm' (*Ibid.*). It is true that, given his stand on the Calas affair, we cannot expect him to be fair to Voltaire. 'Let's leave Calas alone,' he exclaims. 'For an innocent man to perish is just one case of bad luck among many . . .' (vol. i, p. 47). Maistre's successors who were just as hostile to Voltaire were to have the same attitude to Dreyfus at the end of the century.

125 *Mon coeur mis à nu*, xxix and xxx, *Oeuvres complètes*, ed. Le Dantec, Pléiade, 1954, p. 1216.

126 *Discours de la Méthode* (1637), second part.

127 **Diderot**

Oeuvres complètes, ed. Assézat et Tourneux, Garnier, Paris, 1875–7, 20 vols., referred to as A.–T. A new edition which will be a collective effort is at present being published. *Correspondance*, ed. G.Roth, Ed. de Minuit, In course of publication. Fourteen vols. already out. *Lettres à Sophie Volland*, ed. Babelon, Gallimard, 1938, 2 vols., referred to as Babelon. *Oeuvres philosophiques*, ed. Vernière, Garnier, 1956, referred to as Vernière. *Diderot: Interpreter of Nature*, selected writings tr. J.Stewart and J.Kemp, 2nd edn., International Publishers (N.Y.), 1963. *Diderot's Selected Writings*, ed. L.G.Crocker, tr. D.Coltman, Macmillan (N.Y.),

Collier-Macmillan (London), 1966. *Jacques the Fatalist and His Master*, tr., intro, and notes by J.R.Loy, New York University Press, 1959. *The Nun*, tr. M.Sinclair, New English Library, 1966.

O.E.Fellows and N.L.Torrey, *Diderot Studies*, Syracuse University Press, 1949 et seq. R.J.Loy, *Diderot's Determined Fatalist: A Critical Appreciation of 'Jacques le Fataliste'*, King's Crown Press, 1950. L.G. Crocker, *The Embattled Philosopher*, Neville Spearman, 1954.

128 Article on the *Encyclopédie*, A.–T., vol. 14, p. 420.
129 Pensée XXI, Vernière, p. 22-3.
130 LVIII, Questions, Vernière, pp. 241 and 242.
131 Vernière, p. 264.
132 *Ibid.*, p. 311.
133 Letter to M.Duclos, *Correspondance*, vol. V, p. 141.
134 *Ibid.*, p. 257.
135 *Jacques le Fataliste*, A.–T., vol. VI, p. 180.
136 *Ibid.*, p. 313.
137 Letter of 15 October 1759, Babelon, vol. I, p. 70.
138 *Correspondance de Grimm* . . . , ed. Tourneux, vol. VI, pp. 180–1.
139 Babelon, *loc. cit.*
140 *Jacques le Fataliste*, A.–T., vol. VI, pp. 180-1.
141 Letter of 18 October 1760, *Correspondance*, vol. III, p. 156.
142 *Salon de 1763, Oeuvres esthétiques*, p. 525.
143 Undated fragment, Babelon, vol. II, pp. 273-4.
144 *Paradoxe sur le comédien, Oeuvres esthétiques*, p. 362.
145 *Ibid.*, p. 312.
146 *Ibid.*, p. 313.
147 *Ibid.*, p. 310.
148 *De la poésie dramatique, ibid.*, p. 261.
149 *Sur le génie, ibid.*, p. 20.
150 *De la poésie dramatique, ibid.*, p. 284.
151 A.–T., vol. VI, p. 181.
152 *Correspondance de Grimm* . . . , vol. VI, p. 70. 'M.Diderot [is comparable] to a torrent whose impetuous and swift-flowing drive, etc.'.
153 *Salon de 1767, Oeuvres esthétiques, ed. cit.*, pp. 509–10.
154 Letter of 31 August 1769, *Correspondance*, vol. IX, pp. 126–7.
155 Edn. Fabre, p. 59.
156 *Ibid.*, p. 11.
157 *Ibid.*, p. 40.
158 *Ibid.*, p. 41.
159 *Ibid.*, p. 38.
160 *Ibid.*, p. 25.

161 *Ibid.*, p. 37.

162 *Ibid.*, p. 89.

163 *Entretien entre Diderot et D'Alembert* Vernière, p. 274.

164 Edn. Fabre, p. 107.

165 Preface attached to the *Religieuse,* in the *Correspondance de Grimm.* A.-T., vol. v, p. 179.

166 *Jacques le Fataliste.* A.-T., vol. vi, p. 239.

167 **Rousseau**

Oeuvres complètes, Bibliothèque de la Pléiade, 1959–64, 3 vols. already out (vol. i, autobiographical writings; vol. ii, literary writings; vol. iii, political writings). The following references are to this edition, unless otherwise stated. *Correspondance complète,* ed. J.Leigh, Institut Voltaire, Geneva, in course of publication. *The Political Writings,* ed. C.E. Vaughan, 2 vols., Blackwell, 1962. *The Confessions of J.-J.Rousseau,* ed., revised and prefaced by L.G.Crocker, Pocket Books (N.Y.), 1957. *The Confessions of J.-J.Rousseau,* tr. and intro. by J.M.Cohen, Penguin, 1963. *Confessions, etc.,* 2 vols., Dent, E.P.Dutton, 1960. *Emile for Today: The Emile of J.-J.Rousseau,* selected and tr. W.Boyd, Heinemann, 1956. *Emile,* tr. B.Foxley, Dent, E.P.Dutton, 1955. *The Social Contract, Discourse,* tr. and intro. G.D.H.Cole, Dent, E.P.Dutton, 1955. *The Living Thoughts of Rousseau,* presented by Romain Rolland, Longmans (N.Y.), 1939.

'Jean-Jacques Rousseau', *Yale French Studies,* No. 28, New Haven. G.Endore, *The Heart and the Mind: the Story of Rousseau and Voltaire,* W.H.Allen, 1962. J.H.Broome, *Rousseau: A Study of His Thought,* Edward Arnold, 1963. M.Einaudi, *The Early Rousseau,* Cornell University Press, 1967. R.Grimsley, *Rousseau and the Religious Quest,* Clarendon Press, 1968. *Jean-Jacques Rousseau,* L.G.Crocker, Macmillan (N.Y.), 1968-9, 2 vols.

168 Preface to *Narcisse, Oeuvres complètes,* vol. ii, p. 962, footnote.

169 *Confessions,* second part, book ix, vol. i, pp. 402–3.

170 *Lettre à Christophe de Beaumont, Oeuvres complètes,* Didot, 1801, vol. viii, p. 4.

171 *Rousseau, juge de Jean-Jacques,* second dialogue, vol. i Pléiade, p. 850, footnote.

172 *Confessions,* second part, book viii, vol. i, p. 351.

173 *Ibid.,* book ix, vol. i, p. 416.

174 *Lettre à Christophe de Beaumont, ed. cit.,* p. 5.

175 *Ibid.,* p. 14.

176 *Discours sur les Sciences et les Arts* (1750), *Oeuvres complètes,* vol. iii,

p. 28 and footnote (for this quotation and the following two).

177 *Etudes de la Nature,* XII, Didot, 1776, vol. III, pp. 89–94.

178 Reply to Stanislas (on the 1750 *Discours*), *Oeuvres complètes,* vol. III, p. 42.

179 *Discours* (1750), vol. III, p. 30.

180 *Emile,* book I, *Oeuvres complètes* (Didot), vol. VI, p. 29.

181 *Ibid.,* p. 72.

182 *Ibid.,* p. 52.

183 *Ibid.,* book VIII, p. 252.

184 *Ibid.,* p. 330.

185 *Ibid.,* p. 331.

186 *Confessions,* book XI, (at the beginning).

187 *Nouvelle Héloise,* second part, letter XXI.

188 *Ibid.*

189 Testimony of Bernardin de Saint-Pierre, *La vie et les ouvrages de J.-J. Rousseau,* ed. Souriau, Cornély, 1907, p. 56.

190 *Confessions,* second part, book VIII, *Oeuvres complètes,* Pléiade, vol. I, pp. 358–9.

191 Barante, *De la littérature française pendant le XVIIIe siècle,* 1809, ed. of 1822, Ladvocat, p. 244.

192 Seventh *Promenade, Oeuvres complètes,* vol. I, p. 1062.

193 Eighth *Promenade* (at the end).

194 First *Promenade* (at the beginning).

195 Second part, *Oeuvres complètes,* Pléiade, vol. III, p. 170.

196 *Oeuvres choisies,* Leblanc, vol. XXXII, p. V.

Acknowledgments

Acknowledgments – further to any made in the captions – is due to the following for illustrations (the number refers to the page on which the illustration appears): 2, 10, 15, 16, 25, 37, 53, 54, 63, 64, 67, 69, 77, 84, 105, 113, 120-1, 124, 128, 149, 154-5, 162, 165, 181, 189 Hachette; 17, 26, 45, 70, 72-3, 83, 87, 95, 116, 137, 138-9, 171, 175, 194, 199, 207, 223 Photographie Bulloz; 50-1 Dulwich College, London; 88 Courtauld Institute; 131, 145, 214 Mansell Collection; 136 National Gallery, London.

Index

251

World University Library

Titles already published